DK EYEWITNESS TRAVEL

TOP 10
MADRID

CHRISTOPHER & MELANIE RICE

Penguin
Random
House

Top 10 Madrid Highlights

The Top 10 of Everything

CONTENTS

Madrid Area by Area

Streetsmart

Within each Top 10 list in this book, no hierarchy of quality or popularity is implied. All 10 are, in the editor's opinion, of roughly equal merit.

Front cover and spine *Statue of King Philip III in Plaza Mayor, Madrid*
Back cover *Gran Via, Madrid*
Title page *Teatro Real Opera House*

Welcome to
Madrid

Located right in the heart of Spain, Madrid's attractions include world-class art, a lavish royal palace, glorious gardens and showpiece squares. It's a place that fizzes with energy and creativity, yet preserves plenty of old-fashioned appeal. Contemporary art, dance and theatre thrive, while traditional festivals bring *Madrileños* out in droves.

For all Madrid's big-city bustle and glamour, it still feels surprisingly intimate, thanks to the distinct neighbourhood appeal of its different districts, and the friendliness of its inhabitants. Swanky **Salamanca** has the fanciest restaurants and fashion boutiques, while **La Latina** boasts the fantastic **El Rastro** flea market and atmospheric tapas bars. Gritty **Lavapiés** is great for vintage stores and underground bars, while boho-chic **Chueca**'s cocktail bars and cafés feature regularly on the pages of glossy magazines.

You can walk in the footsteps of great writers such as Lope de Vega and Cervantes in the **Barrio de las Letras**; visit a splendid convent for blue-blooded nuns, the **Monasterio de las Descalzas Reales**; picnic under the cherry blossom in the **Parque Quinto de los Molinos**; or watch the sun set over the **Guadarrama mountains**. Shiver at Goya's "Black Paintings" in the **Prado**, or Picasso's *Guernica* in the **Museo Nacional Centro de Arte Reina Sofía**, and try to interpret the enigmatic smile of the Lady of Elche in the **Archaeological Museum**. Once night falls, don't forget that *Madrileños* aren't known as *gatos* (cats) for nothing: you'll dine late and party late in this city that never sleeps.

Whether you are visiting for a weekend or a week, our Top 10 guide is designed to bring together the best of everything the city can offer. It gives you tips throughout, from seeking out what's free to avoiding the crowds, plus nine easy-to-follow itineraries, designed to combine a clutch of sights in a short space of time. Add inspiring photography and detailed maps, and you've got the essential pocket-sized travel companion. **Enjoy the book, and enjoy Madrid.**

Clockwise from top: **View from Palacio de Cibeles; Old Madrid café; Catedrale de la Almudena;** park with almond blossoms; Museo Nacional Centro de Arte Reina Sofía; bridge over Rio Manzanares

Exploring Madrid

Madrid packs in a fantastic array of museums and monuments, parks and gardens, plus great shopping, dining and nightlife. You'll be spoiled for choice for things to do, whatever your interests and however long you spend in the city. Here are some ideas for two and four days of sightseeing and fun in beautiful Madrid.

Plaza Mayor is the city's grandest and most famous square.

Key
— Two-day itinerary
— Four-day itinerary

Two Days in Madrid

Day ❶
MORNING
Enjoy a coffee on the **Plaza Mayor** (see pp22–3), Madrid's showcase square, before strolling east to the Paseo del Prado and the magnificent **Museo Nacional del Prado** (see pp16–21). There's too much to see in one visit, so select some highlights.

AFTERNOON
After lunch, head to **Parque del Retiro** (see pp36–7) to enjoy a stroll through the beautiful gardens, before walking down to the **Museo Nacional Centro de Arte Reina Sofía** (see pp32–5) to see Spain's premier collection of modern art.

Day ❷
MORNING
Take a guided tour of the **Monasterio de las Descalzas Reales** (see pp24–5), a sumptuously decorated 16th-century convent for blue-blooded nuns, then stop at the **Mercado de San Miguel** (see p105) for lunch.

AFTERNOON
Sip a coffee on the handsome **Plaza de Oriente** (see p103), before heading into the **Palacio Real** (see pp12–15), one of the largest places in Europe.

Four Days in Madrid

Day ❶
MORNING
Head out early to Madrid's biggest attraction, the **Prado** (see pp16–21). Spend the morning admiring one of the world's finest collections of European artworks, and don't miss Goya's "Black Paintings", or *Las Meninas* by Velázquez.

AFTERNOON
Amble through the narrow streets of Madrid's historic heart to the elegant **Plaza Mayor** (see pp22–3), then visit the opulent, aristocratic convent of **Monasterio de las Descalzas Reales** (see pp24–5).

Day ❷
MORNING
Spend a morning with the enigmatic Lady of Elche and other archaeological gems at the **Museo**

Parque del Retiro offers a leafy escape from the bustle of the city, with a boating lake, formal gardens and entertainment for all generations.

CHUECA

Museo Arqueológico Nacional

RECOLETOS

Mallorca

Museo Thyssen-Bornemisza

Parque del Retiro

Paseo del Prado

Museo Nacional del Prado

CORTES

Atocha Metro Station

Museo Nacional Centro de Arte Reina Sofía

0 metres 500
0 yards 500

El Escorial is a magnificent complex of royal palace, basilica and monastery.

Arqueológico Nacional *(see pp38–9)*. Then pick up some picnic goodies, perhaps at **Pasteleria Mallorca** *(see p88)*, and head for the gardens of the **Parque del Retiro** *(see pp36–7)*.

AFTERNOON
The serene early Italian Madonnas and works by the French Impressionists provide soothing company at the **Museo Thyssen-Bornemisza** *(see pp28–31)*, and the garden café is an idyllic spot for refreshment and a rest afterwards.

Day ❸
MORNING
If you're in Madrid on a Sunday, make an early visit to the **El Rastro** flea market *(see pp26–7)*. Spend the rest of the morning in the extravagant **Palacio Real** *(see pp12–15)*, whose gilded salons are decorated with exquisite paintings and tapestries.

AFTERNOON
Visit the **Museo Nacional Centro de Arte Reina Sofía** *(see pp32–5)* to admire Picasso's masterpiece, *Guernica*, along with works by Dalí, Miró, Gris, and contemporary artists including Eduardo Arroyo and Miquel Barceló.

Day ❹
MORNING AND AFTERNOON
Spend the whole day at the splendid royal monastery, basilica and palace complex of **El Escorial** *(see pp40–43)*. Between admiring the surprisingly simple apartments, the ornate basilica and the magnificent library, head for the glorious gardens to enjoy a picnic (if you come prepared), or a late lunch afterwards at one of the restaurants in San Lorenzo de El Escorial *(see p130)*.

Top 10 Madrid Highlights

**Boating lake and monument to
Alfonso XII at Parque del Retiro**

🔟 Madrid Highlights

Madrid's three world-class art museums and two royal palaces alone would set pulses racing, but there is more to this exciting and diverse capital than its tourist sights, from the high-fashion boutiques of Salamanca to Madrid's world-famous tapas. To simply watch the world go by, head for the supremely elegant Plaza Mayor.

1 Palacio Real
Once the former residence of Spain's Bourbon rulers, there's something here for everyone *(see pp12–15)*.

2 Museo Nacional del Prado
This world-famous gallery is Madrid's quintessential must-see, with outstanding collections *(see pp16–21)*.

3 Plaza Mayor
This magnificent square, now lined with shops, has been the focal point of the city for centuries *(see pp22–3)*.

4 Monasterio de las Descalzas Reales
This royal convent was founded in the 16th century for the daughters of the aristocracy, whose wealthy families donated many fabulous works of art *(see pp24–5)*.

5 Museo Thyssen-Bornemisza
Madrid was the envy of the world when it outbid the Getty Foundation and others for this priceless collection of European art, which attracts three-quarters of a million visitors every year *(see pp28–31)*.

7 Museo Reina Sofía

No visitor should miss Picasso's *Guernica*, the world's most famous 20th-century painting. This fabulous museum also show-cases many other modern Spanish greats *(see pp32–5)*.

6 El Rastro

The roots of Madrid's famous flea market go back more than 400 years *(see pp26–7)*.

8 Parque del Retiro

Once the preserve of royalty, this beautiful park in the heart of the city is now enjoyed by visitors and *Madrileños* (natives) alike *(see pp36–7)*.

9 Museo Arqueológico Nacional

This vast archaeological museum is home to over 300,000 dazzling art-works and artifacts, now displayed to best effect in a superbly renovated setting *(see pp38–9)*.

10 El Escorial

Set against the stunning backdrop of the Sierra de Guadarrama mountains, Felipe II's awe-inspiring palace, basilica and monastery complex was founded as a mausoleum for Spain's Habsburg rulers *(see p40–43)*.

CHUECA

PASEO DE RECOLETOS

RECOLETOS

PLAZA DE LA CIBELES

PLAZA DE LA INDEPENDENCIA

CALLE DE SERRANO

9

CALA

CARRERA DE SAN JERONIMO

PASEO DEL PRADO

5

PLAZA DE CANOVAS DEL CASTILLO

CORTES

PASEO DEL PRADO

2

CALLE DE ALFONSO XII

CALLE DE

8

CALLE DE ATOCHA

PLAZA DEL EMPERADOR CARLOS V

DE ARGUMOSA

7

| 0 metres | 500 |
| 0 yards | 500 |

Guadarrama

Collado Villalba

10

Las Rozas de Madrid

M505

M503

Madrid

Villaverde

| 0 km | 20 |
| 0 miles | 10 |

TOP 10 ⭐ Palacio Real

Madrid's fabulous Royal Palace is one of Europe's outstanding architectural monuments. More than half of the state apartments are open to the public, sumptuously decorated with silk wall hangings, frescoes and gilded stucco, and crammed with priceless objets d'art. The palace's setting is equally breathtaking: beyond the main courtyard (Plaza de la Armería) lies an uninterrupted vista of park and woodland, stretching to the majestic peaks of the Sierra de Guadarrama.

Façade ①
Stand for a few moments on Plaza de Oriente to enjoy the splendour of Sacchetti's façade **(right)**, gleaming in the sun. Sacchetti achieved a rhythm by alternating Ionic columns with Tuscan pilasters.

③ Hall of Columns
Once the setting for balls and banquets, this room is still used for ceremonial occasions, with Giaquinto's fresco of Carlos III (shown as the sun god Apollo) and superb 17th-century silk tapestries.

② Main Staircase
When Napoleon first saw the exquisite frescoes on the staircase **(above)** after installing his brother on the Spanish throne, he said "Joseph, your lodgings will be better than mine".

Throne Room ④
This room **(right)** was designed for Charles III by Giovanni Battista Natale as a glorification of the Spanish monarchy. The bronze lions that guard the throne were made in Rome in 1651.

NEED TO KNOW
MAP J3 ■ Calle Bailén ■ 91 454 8800 ■ www.patrimonionacional.es

Open Apr–Sep: 10am–8pm daily; Oct–Mar: 10am–6pm daily; 24 & 31 Dec: 10am–2pm closed 18, 29 & 30 Nov, 25 Dec

■ Dis. access ■ Adm €11, €6 (concessions), €7 (for a guided tour including visit to picture gallery), free Mon & Thu (Apr–Sep: 6–8pm; Oct–Mar: 4–6pm) for EU citizens

■ The palace can close for official ceremonies without prior warning, so check before you set out. The best time to avoid the queues is early in the morning.

■ On the first Wednesday of the month (Oct–Jul) you can see the grand Changing of the Guard ceremony at noon. On all other Wednesdays there's a simple ceremony from 11am until 2pm.

5 Gasparini Room

Named after its Italian creator, this dazzling room **(left)** was Charles III's robing room. The lovely ceiling, encrusted with stuccoed fruit and flowers, is a superb example of 18th-century *chinoiserie*.

Plan of Palacio Real

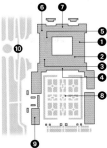

8 The Royal Library

Founded by King Felipe V in 1712, the Royal Library contains more than 20,000 articles, including Isabel I of Castile's *Book of Hours*, a Bible which belonged to Doña María de Molina, and a volume of Scriptures from the era of Alfonso XI of Castile.

9 Armoury

The royal armoury boasts more than 2,000 pieces, mostly made for jousts and tournaments rather than for the battlefield, as well as instruments of torture dating from the days of the Spanish Inquisition.

10 Jardines del Campo del Moro

These gardens were landscaped in the 19th century and planted with acacias, chestnuts, magnolias, cedars and palms. Stand on the avenue to be rewarded with views of the palace's façade.

6 Gala Dining Room

The banqueting hall **(above)** was created for the wedding of Alfonso XII in 1879. The tapestries and ceiling frescoes are by Anton Mengs and Diego Velázquez. Look out for the Chinese vases "of a thousand flowers" in the window recesses.

7 Royal Chapel

Ventura Rodríguez is usually credited with the decoration of this chapel, although he worked hand-in-hand with other collaborators. The dome, supported by massive columns of black marble, is illuminated with some more of Giaquinto's frescoes.

BUILDING THE PALACE

The palace stands on the site of the Alcázar, the 9th-century Muslim castle. In 1734 the wooden structure burned down and Philip V commissioned Italian architect Filippo Juvarra, then Giovanni Sachetti, to design a replacement. Work began in 1738 and was completed in 1764. However, the present king Felipe VI prefers to live at the Palacio de la Zarzuela outside the city.

Art Treasures in the Palacio Real

 Stradivarius Violins
The priceless "Palace Quartet" (two violins, a viola and violoncello) was made in the 18th century by the world-famous luthier, Antonio Stradivari.

2 Vertumnus and Pomona Tapestries
These exquisite tapestries in the Gala Dining Room were made in Brussels by Willem de Panne-maker in the mid-16th century.

3 Porcelain
Among the royal porcelain are some fine examples of Sèvres and Meissen dinnerware.

Tapestry of St John, Hall of Columns

 Tapestries in the Hall of Columns
These 16th-century tapestries depict scenes from the lives of the Apostles.

5 Goya Portraits
The quartet of portraits by Goya depicting Carlos IV and his wife Maria Luisa show the queen as a Spanish *maja* (beauty).

6 Table of the Sphinxes
This 18th-century piece in the Hall of Columns has six bronze sphinxes as table supports.

7 Chronos Clock
Made for Carlos IV in 1799, this contains a marble sculpture of Chronos, representing time.

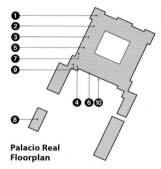

Palacio Real Floorplan

8 Boabdil's Dagger
This beautiful jewelled dagger in the Armoury belonged to the 15th-century Muslim ruler Muhammad XII, also known as Boabdil.

9 Giaquinto's Apollo
Corrado Giaquinto's fresco on the ceiling of the Hall of Columns depicts Carlos III as the sun god Apollo, riding in his chariot across the heavens.

10 Grandeur and Power of the Spanish Monarchy
Giovanni Battista Tiepolo's frescoes in the Throne Room are a *tour de force*. Marginal figures represent Spain's overseas possessions.

Tiepolo's frescoes, Throne Room

THE HABSBURGS AND THE BOURBONS

The Austrian house of Habsburg ruled Spain for nearly 200 years (1516–1700), beginning with Carlos I (Emperor Charles V) and his son Felipe II *(see p43)*. By the time the first Bourbon king, Felipe V (grandson of Louis XIV of France), came to the throne, Spain

Carlos III, an admired and successful ruler

was already in decline. Felipe was immediately challenged by the Habsburg Archduke Charles of Austria, causing the disastrous War of the Spanish Succession (1701–14) which led to Spain losing territories in Belgium, Luxembourg, Italy, Sardinia and Gibraltar. The Bourbon presence also gave Napoleon the excuse to interfere in Spanish affairs, eventually imposing his brother as king. Although the Bourbons were restored (1814), more than a century of political turmoil followed, during which the dynasty's right to rule was continually challenged until the monarchy was abolished in 1931. After the death of the dictator General Franco, in 1975, his nominated successor, the Bourbon King Juan Carlos I, presided over the restoration of democracy, until he abdicated in favour of his son Felipe VI in June 2014.

TOP 10
HABSBURG AND BOURBON RULERS

1 **Carlos I** (1516–56)
2 **Felipe II** (1556–98)
3 **Felipe III** (1598–1621)
4 **Felipe V** (1724–46)
5 **Carlos III** (1759–88)
6 **Carlos IV** (1788–1808)
7 **Fernando VII** (1813–33)
8 **Isabel II** (1833–68)
9 **Alfonso XIII** (1902–31)
10 **Juan Carlos I** (1975–2014)

The Battle of Turin, 1706, by Joseph Parrocel; a key point in the War of the Spanish Succession

TOP 10 ⭐ Museo Nacional del Prado

One of the world's finest art galleries, the Prado has at its core the fabulous Royal Collection of mainly 16th- and 17th-century paintings. Its strongest suit is Spanish painting: artists include Goya with 114 paintings on display, and Velázquez with 50. Highlights of the Italian collection include masterpieces by Fra Angelico, Raphael, Botticelli, Titian and Tintoretto. The Prado owns more than 90 works by Rubens, and canvases by other leading Flemish and Dutch artists. A wing designed by Spanish architect Rafael Moneo, in the restored cloister of the Jerónimos monastery, hosts temporary exhibitions and Renaissance sculpture from the permanent collection.

1 St Dominic Presiding over an Auto-de-Fé

Spanish artist Pedro Berruguete (c.1445–1503) was influenced by the Italians. This painting from around 1495 shows St Dominic sitting in judgment with members of the Inquisition.

3 Jacob's Dream

José de Ribera (1591-1652) reveals his mastery in Jacob's Dream **(right)**, a painting relating to Jacob the Patriarch's mysterious dream as told in the Genesis. This artwork (c.1639) displays José's excellent compositional ability and his delicate sense of colour.

4 Nude Maja

This famous portrait (c.1795–1800) by Francisco Goya (1746–1828) is one of the rare examples of a nude in a Spanish painting of the time. It is one of a pair – the *Clothed Maja* is in the same room for comparison.

6 Las Meninas

This virtuoso exercise in perspective (1656) is by Diego Velázquez (1599–1660). Flanking the Infanta Margarita **(below)** are two ladies-in-waiting (*las Meninas*). The scene also includes the artist, with paintbrush and palette in hand.

2 The Adoration of the Shepherds

Born in Crete, El Greco (1541–1614) was given his nickname ("The Greek") after settling in Toledo in 1577. This inspirational 1612 masterpiece **(above)** was intended for his own tomb.

5 Holy Family with Little Bird

Like his contemporary Francisco de Zurbarán, Bartolomé Esteban Murillo (1617–82) worked in and around Seville, mainly in the decoration of convents and monasteries. This beautiful work (1650), painted with fluent brushstrokes, is typical of his style.

7 The Spinners
This painting **(above)** (c.1657) by Velázquez is an allegory based on the legend of the weaver Arachne.

8 St Jerome
José de Ribera (1591–1652) painted this 1615 depiction of St Jerome in 1644. Like many Spanish artists of the period, Ribera was influenced by Caravaggio.

9 The Meadow of St Isidore
This 1788 Goya landscape brilliantly evokes the atmosphere of the San Isidro celebrations (see p74) and the clear light of spring.

10 The Third of May 1808: The Shootings on Príncipe Pio Hill
In this dramatic 1814 painting, Goya captures the execution of the leaders of the ill-fated insurrection against the French. The illuminated, Christ-like figure (see p19) represents the spirit of freedom being mowed down by the forces of oppression.

NEED TO KNOW

MAP F5 ■ Paseo del Prado ■ 91 330 2800; for advance tickets call 902 10 70 77 ■ www.museodelprado.es

Open 10am–8pm Mon–Sat, 10am–7pm Sun & public hols; 6 Jan, 24 & 31 Dec: 9am–2pm; closed 1 Jan, 1 May, 25 Dec

■ Adm €14, €7 (concessions), adm & guide book €23, free 6–8pm Mon–Sat, 5–7pm Sun ■ Dis. access

■ There's a museum shop, restaurant and café, which is useful as you can easily spend all day in the Prado.

■ To visit all of Madrid's art highlights buy a ticket for the Art Walk (El Paseo del Arte), a combined ticket for the Prado, the Thyssen-Bornemisza (see pp28–31) and the Reina Sofía (see pp32–5). It's available at all three museums and costs €25.60.

MUSEUM GUIDE
The main upper and lower Goya entrances have ticket vending machines outside and ticket desks inside. For disabled access, use the Los Jerónimos entrance. In the Villanueva Building, the second floor has paintings from 1700 to 1800; paintings from 1550 to 1810 are on the first floor; paintings from 1100 to 1910 and sculptures are on the ground floor; and decorative arts are in the basement. The Jerónimos Building has sculptures and temporary exhibitions.

Key to Floorplan
■ Second floor
■ First floor
■ Ground floor

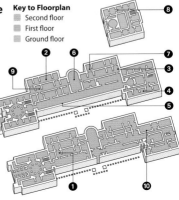

Italian Paintings in the Prado

Death of the Virgin by Mantegnna

Italian Paintings Floorplan

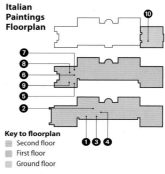

Key to floorplan
- Second floor
- First floor
- Ground floor

1 **Annunciation**
This superb panel (c.1428) by Fra Angelico (c.1400–55) was given to the Monasterio de las Descalzas Reales *(see pp24–5)*.

2 **Death of the Virgin**
This 1460 painting by Andrea Mantegna (c.1431–1506) depicts the last moments of the Virgin Mary's life.

3 **The Story of Nastagio degli Onesti**
These panels (1483) by Botticelli (c.1444–1510) were commissioned by two rich Florentine families.

4 **Portrait of a Cardinal**
This painting (c.1510) by Raphael (1483–1520) is notable for its striking use of colour.

5 **Christ washing the Disciples' feet**
This early work (1547) by Jacopo Tintoretto (c.1518–94) reveals his brilliant handling of perspective.

6 **Danäe and the Shower of Gold**
Paintings by Titian (1488–1576) were prized by Carlos I. This 1553 work depicts a mythological story by Ovid.

7 **David with the Head of Goliath**
Caravaggio (1571–1610) had a major impact on Spanish artists, who admired the dark and light contrasts, as seen here (c.1600).

8 **Madonna and Child between two Saints**
Founder of the Venetian School, Giovanni Bellini (c.1431–1516) shows an assured use of colour in this devotional painting (c.1490).

9 **Venus and Adonis**
This beautiful work (c.1580) by Paolo Veronese (1528–88) is a masterpiece of light and colour.

Venus and Adonis by Paolo Veronese

10 **The Immaculate Conception**
This work (1767–9) by Tiepolo (1696–1770) is one of a series intended for a church in Aranjuez.

GOYA'S "BLACK PAINTINGS"

Portrait of Francisco Goya

Technically brilliant, irreverent, ironic, satirical, sarcastic and bitter, Goya's "black paintings" are some of the most extraordinary works in the history of art. They originally decorated the rooms of his house, the *Quinta del Sordo* (Villa of the Deaf), near the River Manzanares and were produced while he was recovering from a serious illness. In 1873 the then owner of the *Quinta*, Baron D'Erlanger, had the paintings transferred to canvas and donated them to the Prado Museum. What these 14 paintings have in common, apart from the uniformly sombre colour scheme, is a preoccupation with corruption, human misery, sickness and death. The key to the series is the terrifying *Saturn devouring his Son*, which is based on a painting by Rubens, but in which the god is transformed from a Baroque hero to the incarnation of evil. Even *San Isidro Fair*, which features Goya himself, is almost a travesty of his earlier depiction of the festival *(see p17)*, and reveals how far he had travelled as man and artist over the years.

TOP 10
EVENTS IN THE LIFE OF FRANCISCO DE GOYA

1 Born in Fuendetodos, near Zaragoza (1746)

2 Joins workshop of local artist, José Luzán (1760)

3 Moves to Madrid and works at Royal Tapestry Factory (1774)

4 Admitted to San Fernando Academy (1780)

5 Appointed court painter (1786)

6 Becomes deaf (1792)

7 Begins an affair with Duchess of Alba (c.1796)

8 Witnesses failed uprising against the French (1808)

9 Goes into exile in France (1824)

10 Dies in Bordeaux (1828)

The Third of May 1808: The Shootings on Príncipe Pio Hill, Francisco Goya

Flemish and Dutch Paintings

The Descent from the Cross

Flemish and Dutch Paintings Floorplan

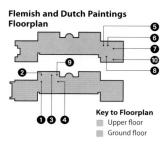

Key to Floorplan

◻ Upper floor
◻ Ground floor

1 The Descent from the Cross

Felipe II hung this beautiful composition (c.1435) by Rogier van der Weyden (1399–1464) in El Escorial *(see pp40–43)*. It was moved here after the Civil War.

2 The Garden of Delights

The meaning of this famous and unsettling work (1500) by Hieronymus Bosch (c.1450–1516) is hotly debated. The traditional view is that it is a warning against earthly pleasures.

3 The Triumph of Death

This terrifying version of the Dance of Death (c.1562–3) is by Flemish master, Pieter Breughel the Elder (c.1525–69).

4 Portrait of Mary Tudor

Antonis Mor (1517–76) painted this superb portrait in 1554 of the 37-year-old Queen of England, who was to marry Felipe II.

5 Judith at the Banquet of Holofernes

This 1634 painting is the only work in the Prado by Rembrandt (1606–69). Judith's maid can be seen carrying the sack into which Judith will later place the head of her enemy, Holofernes.

6 The Painter's Family

Jacob Jordaens (1593–1678) was one of the finest portrait artists of the 17th century, as can be seen in this 1622 painting of himself with his wife and daughter. The painting is full of symbols of marital fidelity.

7 The Artist with Sir Endymion Porter

This double portrait painted from 1632–7 by Antony van Dyck (1599–1641) shows him with the diplomat Endymion Porter, his friend and patron at the court of King Charles I.

8 Adoration of the Magi

Peter Paul Rubens (1577–1640) first painted this in 1609 but returned to it in 1628 to add three strips that included various figures and his self-portrait.

The Three Graces by **Peter Paul Rubens**

9 Landscape with Saint Jerome

This 1516–17 Joachim Patenier (1480–1524) work depicts the saint gently taking out a thorn from the paw of a lion.

10 The Three Graces

This erotic masterpiece (c.1635) by Rubens was inspired by classical sculpture. It features Love, Desire and Virginity, two of them modelled on wives of the artist.

FURTHER EUROPEAN HIGHLIGHTS IN THE PRADO

Self Portrait by Albrecht Dürer, painted in 1498

The highlights of the small but valuable German Collection (room 55B ground floor) are Albrecht Dürer's *Self Portrait*, painted in 1498, one of a quartet of paintings by this Renaissance master, and his depictions of Adam and Eve. Most of the French Collection dates from the 17th and 18th centuries (first floor, rooms 2–4). Outstanding are the landscapes of Claude Lorrain and the work of Nicolas Poussin. Felipe II began collecting Classical sculptures (ground floor, rooms 71–4) in the 16th century, mostly Roman copies of Greek originals. Look out for the three Venuses – Madrid Venus, Venus of the Shell, Venus of the Dolphin – and the priceless San Idefonso Group, dating from the reign of the Emperor Augustus (1st century AD). The Dauphin's Treasure (basement) was inherited by Felipe V, heir presumptive to Louis XIV of France. The fabulous collection of goblets, glasses and serving dishes was made from precious stones (jasper, lapis lazuli, agate and rock crystal) and encrusted with jewels.

TOP 10 EUROPEAN WORKS OF ART

1 Self Portrait, Albrecht Dürer (German Collection)

2 Hunting Party in Honour of Charles V in Torgau, Lucas Cranach the Elder (German Collection)

3 St Paula Romana embarking at Ostia, Claude Lorrain (French Collection)

4 Parnassus, Nicolas Poussin (French Collection)

5 San Idefonso statues (Classical Sculptures)

6 Madrid Venus (Classical Sculptures)

7 Venus of the Shell (Classical Sculptures)

8 Statue of Demeter (Classical Sculptures)

9 Onyx salt cellar with Mermaid (Dauphin's Treasure)

10 The Hunt Vessel (Dauphin's Treasure)

Parnassus by Nicolas Poussin (1594–1665)

Plaza Mayor

Madrid's most famous square, completed in 1619, was built on a grand scale. Capable of holding up to 50,000 people, it was intended to impress, and still does. Nowadays it's a tourist attraction first and foremost: a place for relaxing with a drink and watching the world go by. It was originally known as Plaza de Arrabal ("Outskirts Square") because it lay outside the city walls. Following a fire in 1791, Juan de Villanueva (architect of the Prado) redesigned the square, adding the granite archways that now enclose it. Plaza Mayor has been a market, an open-air theatre, a bullring and a place of execution. Its buildings are now mainly used by the city government.

Statue of Felipe III ①

This magnificent statue **(right)** by two Italian artists, Pietro Tacca and Giambologna, was moved here in the 19th century. Presented to Felipe III in 1616 by the Florentine ruler Cosimo de' Medici, it was originally in the Casa de Campo.

② **Casa de la Panadería**

This house was the headquarters of the bakers' guild, which had great power in controlling the price of grain. The portal survives from the original building which burned down in 1672.

③ **Arco de Cuchilleros**

Cutlers Arch is so called for the sword-makers who once traded here. Today the street is known for taverns such as Las Cuevas de Luis Candelas, named after a 19th-century bandit said to have hidden in its cellars.

④ **Casa de la Panadería Murals**

In the 1980s it was decided that the façade murals of "Bakery House" were beyond saving, and a competition was held for a new design. The winner, Carlos Franco, painted allegories of the zodiac signs in 1992 **(left)**.

⑤ **Arcade Shops**

Buying and selling has always been the life-blood of Plaza Mayor, with shops selling everything from espadrilles to icons. At El Arco de Cuchilleros (No. 9) all the items on sale have been made by local artisans, continuing a centuries-old tradition.

6 Casa de la Carnicería

This building **(above)** was erected in 1617 and was originally the meat market. It is now used by the Central District Government (Junta Municipal del Distrito de Centro).

7 Cava de San Miguel

When the houses were built on this street **(right)** adjacent to Plaza Mayor, huge quantities of earth were removed from the foundations of the square. To prevent its collapse, frontages on the Cava were designed as sloping buttresses.

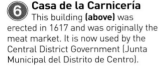

9 Terrace Bars and Cafés

Relaxing over a leisurely drink on an outdoor terrace is the best way to appreciate the square. Look out for the speciality *bocadillo de calamares* (bread roll filled with squid).

10 Stamp and Coin Market

This market takes place every Sunday morning from around 10am to 2pm and attracts amateur and expert collectors from all over Spain.

8 Lampposts

The modern lampposts **(left)** set around the statue of Felipe III are engraved with scenes depicting life on the square in days gone by. They include a masquerade ball, an interrogation by members of the Inquisition and a bullfight.

AUTO-DE-FÉ

The cellars at number 4 of Calle Felipe III were once used by the Inquisition to torture those accused of heresy, witchcraft and a multitude of other crimes. Once condemned, they had to undergo a ceremony known as the auto-de-fé. This macabre spectacle, which included a ritual procession and public humiliations, lasted from dawn to dusk.

🔟 ⭐ Monasterio de las Descalzas Reales

This museum is also a working convent – a haven of peace and quiet after the noise and bustle of Puerta del Sol and the Gran Vía nearby. The building started out as a palace, owned by the royal treasurer, Alonso Gutiérrez, but in 1555 he sold it to the sister of Felipe II, Juana of Austria, who founded the convent four years later. The nuns were Franciscans, but became known, because of their aristocratic backgrounds, as the "Barefoot Royals". The convent is crammed with works of art donated by the nuns' wealthy relatives. The church (rarely open to the public) contains Juana's tomb (1547–1578).

Grand Staircase ①

Nothing prepares visitors for this extraordinary sight. The Grand Staircase **(right)** belongs to the original palace, but the dazzling frescoes and *trompe l'oeil,* covering walls, arches and balustrades, were added in the 17th century.

② Royal Balcony

As you climb the staircase, look right and you'll see another *trompe l'oeil* feature. On the "balcony" are Felipe IV and his family – Mariana of Austria, the Infanta Margarita Teresa and Felipe Prospero, the Prince of Asturias. The prince offers an accurate date for the painting by Antonio Pereda, as he died, aged four, in 1661.

③ Chapel of the Virgin of Guadalupe

The 68 panels by Sebastián Herrera Barnuevo (1619–71) feature matriarchs of the Old Testament. The Virgin of Guadalupe painting is a 16th-century replacement.

Key to Floorplan
- ■ Lower floor
- ■ Ground floor
- ■ First Floor
- ■ Second Floor

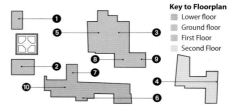

Plan of the Monasterio de las Descalzas Reales

4 Tapestry Room

The magnificent collection of tapestries, on display in the former nuns' dormitories, were made in Brussels in the 17th century. The 10 panels on view represent the Triumph of the Eucharist.

5 Upper Cloister

The tiny chapels surrounding the cloister (above) were rooms of the original palace. Outstanding among the 16th- and 17th-century works of art is a wooden polychrome *Recumbent Christ* by Gaspar Becerra.

6 Hall of Kings

This portrait gallery was once used by members of the royal family as a retreat. Works include this charming portrait (left) by Coello.

7 Chapter House

The highlight here is a series of 16th-century frescoes depicting the life of St Francis of Assisi. Look out for two devotional works by Pedro de Mena: *Ecce Homo* and *Master Dolorosa*.

NEED TO KNOW

MAP M3 ■ Plaza de las Descalzas Reales s/n ■ 91 45 48800 ■ www.patrimonionacional.es

Open 10am–2pm, 4–6:30pm Tue–Sat, 10am–3pm Sun & public hols; closed 24, 25 & 31 Dec ■ Adm €6, free for EU citizens (4–6:30pm) Wed & Thu

■ The guided tour lasts for 1 hour, and it is advisable to book well in advance as places on the tour are limited. While all the commentary is given in Spanish, questions in English are welcomed.

RENAISSANCE MUSIC

Today the convent is famous for its artistic treasures, but in the 16th century it was equally renowned for its music. This was largely due to the reputation of Tomás Luis de Victoria, chaplain to the Empress María from 1586 to his death in 1611. Born in Ávila, Victoria studied music in Rome, but his output is infused with a mysticism more typical of the Spanish Counter-Reformation. Victoria's religious music was among the first to be heard in the New World.

8 Antechoir

Visitors enter through an intricately carved Plateresque doorway. Among the paintings lining the walls of the three chapels is a beautiful *Virgin and Child* from the late 15th century – one of the oldest works of art in the convent.

9 Choir

The choir (above) contains the tombs of Empress María of Austria (sister of Joanna) and the Infanta Margarita. One portrait over the entrance is known as the "abandoned girlfriend" – the sister, María of Portugal, was betrothed to Felipe II but he married Mary Tudor of England instead.

10 Candilón (Funeral Room)

By tradition, when a nun died her body was placed on the tiled bier, while prayers were said under the light of a large lamp (*candil*) (right). The royal portraits include two of Felipe II's children and Juana of Austria, both by the 16th-century artist Alonso Sánchez Coello.

🔟 ⭐ El Rastro

This colourful street market in one of the city's oldest working-class neighbourhoods has been going for much more than 100 years. The word *rastro* means "trail" and refers to the animal innards that were dragged through the streets when this was the site of the main abattoir. Goya immortalized the street types here in paintings such as *The Blind Guitarist*, while earlier the area had been the backdrop for satires by playwrights of the Golden Age. Among the most exotic inhabitants were the amazonas, a team of horsewomen who performed at royal receptions in the 16th century, and are remembered in Calle Amazonas.

① Calle de la Ribera de Curtidores

The Rastro's main street is named after the *curtidores* (tanners) who once plied their trade here. You can still pick up a leather jacket on one of the dozens of stalls **(right)**, as well as T-shirts, belts, handbags and hats.

② Statue of Eloy Gonzalo

At the siege of Cascorro in Cuba (1898) Eloy Gonzalo **(left)** volunteered to start a blaze in the enemy camp and was fatally wounded. Look closely at the statue and you'll see the petrol can.

③ Plaza del General Vara de Rey

Second-hand clothes, candelabras, books and old furniture are on offer in this bustling square.

④ Calle Carlos Arniches

Dropping away from the square, this stall-lined street **(below)** marks the beginning of the flea market proper. The lock vendor and his dog are a regular fixture.

⑤ Calle Mira el Sol

The place to head to if you're after something electrical, including spare parts and mobile phones. The corner with Ribera de Curtidores is the favourite pitch of the *organillera* (lady organ-grinder).

⑥ Calle del Gasómetro

Car owners may find what they're looking for here: there's usually a good selection of anti-theft locks, windscreen wipers, brake lights and tools **(right)**. There's also a brisk trade in computer parts.

9 Eating in El Rastro

There are many bars and cafés in the area. Malacatín **(below)** at Calle de la Ruda 5 rustles up the delicious, meaty local stew *cocido madrileño*.

7 Plaza Campillo del Mundo Nuevo

Adult collectors and children are the main customers, browsing the stacks of old comics and magazines in the vicinity of this square **(above)**. You'll also find CDs, vinyl records, toys and oddities such as binoculars and magnifying glasses.

RÍO MANZANARES

The streets of the Rastro lead down to one of Madrid's most neglected features. The Manzanares River is famous only for being short on water and has been the butt of jokes since time immemorial. Until late in the 19th century, its banks were the haunt of washer-women *(lavanderas)*, colourful figures who appear in the paintings of Francisco Goya. The Baroque bridge dates from 1719–32. In the middle of it are sculptures of Madrid's patron saint, San Isidro.

8 Stalls off Ribera de Curtidores

Painting equipment and picture frames are the speciality of Calle San Cayetano, while stalls near the Army & Navy store on Calle Carnero sell a wide range of sports gear. Pet owners should head for Calle Fray Ceferino González for the miscellany of dog collars, fishing nets and bird cages.

10 Puerta de Toledo

This triumphal arch **(left)** was unveiled in 1827 and dedicated to Fernando VII. It was first proposed during the French occupation to extol the values of liberty and democracy.

NEED TO KNOW

MAP C5 ■ **Open** 8:30am–3pm Sun ■ Dis. access ■ Metro La Latina

■ While Sunday is the main trading day, some stallholders set out their wares on Saturdays, too.

■ The Rastro is a happy hunting ground for thieves and pickpockets so keep a close eye on your valuables at all times.

🔟 ⭐ Museo Thyssen-Bornemisza

One of the most important art collections in the world focuses on European painting from the 13th to the 20th centuries. The wealthy industrialist Baron Heinrich Thyssen-Bornemisza began acquiring Old Masters in the 1920s for his villa in Switzerland. After the baron's death in 1947, his son, Hans Heinrich, added modern masterpieces, including French Impressionists, German Expressionists and the pick of the Russian Avant-Garde to the collection. In 1993 the state bought the 1,000-strong collection for the knock-down price of $350 million (the true value being estimated at nearer $1 billion). In 2005 an extension opened, displaying magnificent Impressionist works.

1 Christ and the Samaritan Woman
Outstanding among the collection of Italian Primitives is this work (1310–11) by Sienese master Duccio di Buoninsegna (c.1278–1319). The painting's life-like quality **(right)** reveals Duccio's interest in accuracy, and looks forward to the Renaissance.

2 Rembrandt's Self-Portrait
This self-portrait (c.1643) by Rembrandt (1606–69) is one of more than 60 such works by the great Dutch artist. It reveals Rembrandt's view of himself as an isolated genius.

3 Young Knight in a Landscape
Vittore Carpaccio (c.1460–1525) is an important representative of the Venetian school. This intriguing work (1510) shows a courtly knight amid symbolic animals and plants **(below)**.

4 View of Alkmaar from the Sea
Dutch Golden Age artist Salomon van Ruysdael's (1600–70) evocative seascape (c.1650) is considered to be one of the finest examples of the genre, for its effortless mastery of colour and perspective.

5 Madonna of the Dry Tree
This devotional painting (c.1450) by Dutch artist Petrus Christus (c.1410–72) was inspired by an Old Testament metaphor in which God brings the dry tree (the chosen people) to life. The "A"s hanging from the tree stand for Ave Maria.

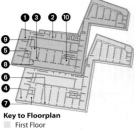

Key to Floorplan
First Floor
Second Floor

9 Portrait of Henry VIII of England

During the 16th century, portraiture was a leading genre. When Hans Holbein, the Younger (c.1497–1543) was in the service of Henry VIII, he depicted the king (c.1537) **(left)** in an almost frontal pose. Henry's rich attire suggests that this was for a private room in Whitehall Palace.

6 Expulsion, Moon and Firelight

This haunting work (c.1828) is by the American Thomas Cole, founder of the Hudson River School. Cole idealized the untrammelled American landscape as a new Garden of Eden.

7 Still Life with Cat and Rayfish

This witty still life (c.1728) in the Dutch style is by the French artist, Jean-Baptiste-Siméon Chardin (1699–1779). Its companion piece, *Still Life with Cat and Fish*, is in Room 27.

8 Portrait of Giovanna Tornabuoni

This sublime portrait (1489) by Florentine artist Domenico Ghirlandaio (1449–94), was the last Baron Thyssen's favourite. It was commissioned to celebrate the marriage of Giovanna degli Albizzi to Lorenzo Tornabuoni – a union of two powerful families. Tragically, Giovanna died in childbirth shortly afterwards.

10 The Annunciation

Distorted figures, swirling lines and bold colours **(below)** are typical of the Mannerist style which El Greco (1541– 1614) mastered in Venice, where he was influenced by Titian and Tintoretto. This intensely spiritual painting (c.1567–1577) reveals the Cretan artist's development following his move to Toledo, Spain, in 1577.

NEED TO KNOW

MAP F4 ▪ Paseo del Prado 8 ▪ 902 760 511 ▪ www.museothyssen.org

Open 10am–7pm Tue–Sun (Jul–Aug: to 11pm Tue–Sat); closed 1 Jan, 1 May, 25 Dec ▪ Adm €10, more for combinations of different collections

(concessions); free Mon noon–4pm ▪ Dis. access

▪ The café-restaurant has magnificent views of the garden.

▪ The Thyssen opens for evening showings in summer, when you can dine at the garden restaurant.

Museum Guide
The collection is organized chronologically, starting with Italian Primitives on the top floor and ending with 20th-century abstract and Pop Art. Temporary exhibitions are held on the ground floor and basement. There is also a viewing terrace on the fifth floor.

Modern Paintings in the Thyssen

Woman with a Parasol in a Garden by Renoir

1 Woman with a Parasol in a Garden

This painting (c.1873) **(above)** is by one of the founders of the influential Impressionist movement, Pierre-Auguste Renoir (1841–1920). Renoir was apprenticed for four years as a porcelain painter, and later attributed his technical brilliance in handling surface and texture to his early training.

2 Swaying Dancer

This exquisite study of a dancer in mid-performance (1877–9) by French artist Edgar Degas (1834–1917) is one of a series of his works devoted to the ballet. Unlike some of his fellow Impressionist painters, Degas placed great emphasis on the importance of drawing, as the superb draughtsmanship of this pastel **(right)** clearly shows.

3 Les Vessenots

Vincent Van Gogh (1853–90) painted this dazzling rural landscape (1890) during the final year of his troubled life. He worked feverishly while staying at Les Vessenots, near Auvers in northern France, producing more than 80 canvases, mostly landscapes, (which were painted outdoors), in less than three months.

4 Fränzi in Front of a Carved Chair

Ernst Ludwig Kirchner (1880–1938) was an important figure in German Expressionism and a member of the group known as Die Brücke (The Bridge), which began the movement in Dresden. These artists were more interested in expressing feelings through their work, and encouraging emotional responses from their audience, rather than portraying outward reality. Fränzi Fehrmann, seen in this lovely work, dating from 1910, was one of their favourite models.

5 The Dream

A founder member, with Wassily Kandinsky, of the influential *Blaue Reiter* (Blue Rider) group, German artist Franz Marc (1880–1916) took Expressionism in a new, spiritual direction. Colours, as in this 1912 work, are used symbolically (blue was masculine and yellow feminine, for example), as are the animals in his paintings, which represent truth, beauty and other ideals.

6 Still Life with Instruments

Liubov Popova (1889–1924) was one of the most innovative artists working in Russia in the period leading up to the

Swaying Dancer, Degas

Revolution. This Cubist painting (1915) **(below)**, completed after a period in Paris, is part of a suite of works called *Painterly Architectonics*, an even bolder example of which is exhibited in Room 41.

Modern Paintings Floorplan

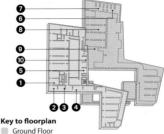

Key to floorplan

▢ Ground Floor
▢ First Floor

Still Life with Instruments, **Popova**

7 New York City

Piet Mondrian (1872–1944) was one of the most influential abstract artists of the 20th century. Born in the Netherlands, he moved to New York after the outbreak of World War II. The simple geometrical forms and bold colours of this abstract painting (1940–42) celebrate the energy and dynamism of his adopted home.

8 Brown and Silver I

Famous for his "action paintings" – random throwing or pouring of paint onto the canvas in an effort to create spontaneity – Jackson Pollock (1912–56) made a huge impact on postwar art in America. This painting (c.1951) is typical of the artist's revolutionary approach to making art.

9 Portrait of Baron H.H. Thyssen-Bornemisza

This revealing study of the museum's benefactor (1981–2) is the work of Britain's most distinguished portrait artist, Lucian Freud (1922–2011). In the background is *Pierrot Content* by Jean-Antoine Watteau (1684–1721), which visitors will find in Room 28.

10 Hotel Room

In this moving 1931 painting **(below)** by American artist Edward Hopper (1882–1967) the bare furnishings, discarded suitcase and disconsolate posture of the woman holding the railway timetable masterfully suggest loneliness and dislocation – a subject the artist returned to repeatedly. Hopper is the most important representative of the American social realist school, created in the wake of the Wall Street Crash of 1929, and the Great Depression that followed.

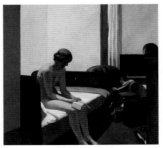

Hotel Room **by Edward Hopper**

TOP10 ⭐ Museo Nacional Centro de Arte Reina Sofía

The Reina Sofía's collection of 20th- and 21st-century Spanish art is exciting and challenging by turns. The museum, set in a former hospital, was inaugurated by King Juan Carlos and Queen Sofía in 1992 and, besides the permanent collection, stages temporary exhibitions. While there are works by the great masters of the interwar period – Juan Gris, Joan Miró, Salvador Dalí and Pablo Picasso, whose *Guernica* is the centrepiece of the gallery *(see p35)* – visitors can also find lesser-known Spanish painters and sculptors.

1 Woman in Blue
This marvellous Blue-period portrait (1901) of an insolent-looking courtesan by Pablo Picasso (1881–1973) was painted from memory soon after his first visit to Paris. When it failed to win a national competition, a disgruntled Picasso discarded it.

2 Shout No. 7
Antonio Saura (1930–1998) portrays the devastation after the Spanish Civil War in this painting (1959). He was a key exponent of the Spanish *art brut* trend which achieved international success in the late 1950s, once the Spanish borders were opened to artists.

3 Portrait of Sonia de Klamery
Hermenegildo Anglada-Camarasa (1871–1959) had a sensual style as this evocative painting (c.1913) shows.

4 The Gathering at the Café de Pombo
José Gutiérrez Solana (1886–1945) loved to record the social life of Madrid, as seen in this 1920 portrait. The painting's owner, Ramón Gómez de la Serna, is shown in the centre **(below)**.

Museo Nacional Centro de Arte Reina Sof

5 Lying Figure
This nude by Francis Bacon (1909–1992) was based on photographs of Henrietta Moraes by John Deakin, and evokes the distortion of humanity.

6 The Great Masturbator
Catalan artist Salvador Dalí (1904–89) was a leading exponent of Surrealism, with its exploration of the subconscious. The figure of the Masturbator (1929) is derived from a weird rock formation at Cadaqués, close to where Dalí had a home.

Accidente 7

Also known as *Self-portrait*, Alfonso Ponce de León's (1906–36) disturbing work **(right)** was painted during the last year of his life, and prefigures his tragic death in a car crash. The painting, which shows a man violently thrown from a vehicle, is a mixture of realistic elements, along with lack of depth, flat colour and artificial lighting, which reflect the artist's use of both Surrealism and Magic Realism.

8 Portrait II

Joan Miró (1893–1983) encompassed Cubism and Surrealism but he never lost his extraordinary originality. In this 1938 work **(right)** the Catalan painter is more interested in juxtaposing colours rather than revealing the physical attributes of the sitter.

9 Superimposition of Grey Matter

Antoni Tàpies's (1923–2012) "matter paintings" explore texture and are composed by adding layers of mixed media, such as sand, powdered marble and paint, onto a pre-varnished canvas.

10 Guitar in Front of the Sea

Juan Gris (1887–1927) became one of Cubism's leading exponents. This 1925 work is an excellent example.

NEED TO KNOW

MAP F6 ■ Calle Santa Isabel 52 ■ 91 774 1000 ■ www.museoreinasofia.es

■ **Open** 10am–9pm Mon & Wed–Sat, 10am– 7pm Sun; closed Tue, 1 Jan, 6 Jan, 1 May, 15 May, 9 Nov, 24–25 Dec, 31 Dec ■ Adm €8 (free 7–9pm Mon & Wed–Sat, 1:30–7pm Sun); Paseo del Arte €25.60

■ Disabled access

■ The café-restaurant on the ground floor of the Nouvel Building has a daily set-price menu and is accessed from the museum, or from Calle Argumosa 43.

■ The museum shop sells Spanish designer jewellery and ceramics as well as books, slides and posters.

Museum Guide
The entrance to the main Sabatini Building is in Plaza Sánchez Bustillo. Permanent collections can be found on the first, second and fourth floors, and temporary exhibitions on the first and third floors. Further permanent collections are in the Nouvel Building. Exhibits are susceptible to change. To the west and south of the courtyard are two buildings housing an art library, a restaurant, a book shop and an auditorium.

Sculptures in the Reina Sofía

1 Daphne

From the mid-1920s, Julio González (1876–1942) developed a sculpting language by working with metals using industrial construction methods. *Daphne* (1937) is a defining piece that show-cases the possibilities that this new artistic language had to offer.

2 Great Prophet

Catalan artist Pablo Gargallo (1881–1934) was one of the most important Spanish sculptors during the 1920s and 1930s. He spent nearly 30 years planning this 1933 masterpiece which was cast sadly only after his death.

3 Portrait of Joella

This beautiful sculpture-painting (1933–4) was the fruit of a collaboration between Catalan Salvador Dalí and the leading American Surrealist, Man Ray (1890–1976). Man Ray fashioned the head, leaving Salvador Dalí to add the striking painted dream landscape across the face.

4 Seated Woman I

Born in Barcelona, Julio González (1876–1942) became an apprentice, first in his father's metalsmith shop and then as welder in Paris, and his training at the forge had a major impact on his work. This abstract piece from c.1935 is very typical of his output.

Seated Woman I

5 Man with a Lamb

This 1943 work by Pablo Picasso is a traditional sculpture in the manner of Rodin. Picasso's studies of the period suggest that the lamb is a symbol of sacrifice.

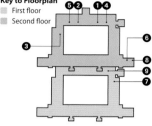

Key to Floorplan

☐ First floor
☐ Second floor

6 Sailor with Guitar

Born in Lithuania, Jacques Lipchitz (1891–1973) fell under the spell of Cubism during his first stay in Paris in 1909. This piece (1917) is representative of his Cubist sculptures.

7 Empty Suspension

Jorge de Oteiza (1908–2003) was a highly original Basque sculptor. This forged steel sculpture (1957) was developed around the time the artist was taking an interest in American megalithic statuary.

8 Bather

Spanish sculptor Mateo Hernández (1884–1949) produced work influenced by Art Deco and New Objectivity trends during the interwar years. *Bather* (1925) follows the Ancient Greek style of being carved in coral granite.

9 Woman in the Garden

In the late 1920s, Picasso frequented the studio of Catalan artist Julio González in Paris, and was inspired to develop his own metal sculpting techniques. Results include this remarkable bronze *Woman in the Garden* (1930–32).

10 Toki Egin (Homage to St John of the Cross)

Eduardo Chillida (1924–2002) is one of Spain's most highly regarded sculptors. This huge iron work (1989–90) weighs 9,000 kg (17,500 lbs) – cranes were used to install it in the garden.

PABLO PICASSO'S GUERNICA

Spanish town of Guernica, after the bombing by German and Italian aircraft in 1937

On display in Room 206 of the museum is its most precious and famous work. Commissioned as propaganda, *Guernica* instantly transcended its original purpose. In April 1937, at the height of the Civil War, German bombers devastated the Basque town of Guernica (Gernika) in support of General Franco's Nationalist forces. The attack, almost unprecedented, on a defenceless civilian population, caused international outrage. Picasso completed his huge canvas in just two months and it was first exhibited at the Paris World's Fair. Ever since, the meaning and content of *Guernica* have been minutely analysed, to the irritation of the artist. Picasso chose not to depict the bombardment – there are no airplanes, for example – but to indict war, with all its senselessness and barbarity, conceived in terms of the artist's highly individual language of symbols. The preliminary sketches (some of which are on display in the adjacent rooms) help the viewer to understand the work. Picasso tried eight different versions before arriving at his ultimate vision.

TOP 10 FEATURES IN PICASSO'S GUERNICA

1 Bull

2 Wounded Horse

3 Bereaved Mother

4 Dead Child

5 Dead Soldier

6 Candle

7 Light Bulb

8 Broken Dagger

9 Window

10 Eyes

***Guernica*'s symbolism** of dismembered bodies, staring eyes, rearing horses gripped in pain, and desperate outstretched arms, combined with the bleakness of a mono-chrome colour scheme, express the artist's view of war.

🔟 ⭐ Parque del Retiro

The Retiro is the city's green lung and the *Madrileños'* favourite weekend retreat. The aristocracy was admitted to the former royal grounds in 1767 but it was another century before the gates were opened to the general public. Visitors can enjoy the decorative features, which include statues, follies, a formal French garden and a boating lake, as well as the numerous amenities. Children will make a beeline for the puppet theatre, while adults may prefer the concerts at the bandstand. Sunday, when there is almost a carnival atmosphere, is the best day to enjoy everything from circus acts and buskers to pavement artists and fortune-tellers.

Estanque ❶

The boating lake **(right)** is one of the oldest features of the park (1631). In the days of Felipe IV, it was the setting for mock naval battles. Rowing boats are available for hire from the jetty. Once in a while the lake is drained for cleaning and 6,000 fish have to find a temporary home.

❷ Puerta de la Independencia

The handsome Independence Gate **(below)** does not rightfully belong here. It was designed by Antonio López Aguado as the entrance to a palace built by Fernando VII for his second wife, Isabel de Bragança. It is, however, the most important of the 18 gates.

Monument to Alfonso XII ❸

This huge monument **(below)** was conceived in 1898 as a defiant response to Spain's humiliating defeat in Cuba, but the plans were not realized until 1922. The equestrian statue of the king is by Mariano Benlliure. The most impressive feature is the handsome curved colonnade, lined with bronze sculptures. It is a popular spot with sun-worshippers.

Plan of the Parque del Retiro

4 Palacio de Velázquez
The Retiro's exhibition centre is the work of Ricardo Velázquez Bosco. The tiled frieze perfectly offsets the pink and yellow brick banding (above).

5 Paseo de las Estatuas
This line of Baroque statues, representing the kings and queens of Spain, other Iberian rulers and Aztec chief, Montezuma, was intended to impress.

7 Casita del Pescador
The "fisherman's house", a typical of the era *capricho* (whim), was a part of the re-landscaping of the park in the 1820s. A water-wheel, concealed by the grotto and artificial hill, creates a cascade.

8 Fuente de la Alcachofa
The "artichoke fountain" was designed by Ventura Rodríguez, and made of Sierra de Guadarrama granite and Colmenar stone. The artichoke at the top is supported by four cherubs.

9 El Ángel Caído
This beguiling sculpture (right), the work of Ricardo Bellver, is said to be the only public monument to the "fallen angel" (Lucifer) in the world. It was unveiled in 1878.

10 Palacio de Cristal
Mirrored in a lake and framed by trees, the Crystal Palace was inspired by its British namesake in 1887.

6 Rosaleda
The rose garden (above) holds more than 4,000 roses representing 100 different varieties. Designed by the city's head gardener, Cecilio Rodríguez, in 1915, it is modelled on the Bagatelle in the Bois de Boulogne, Paris.

🔟 ⭐ Museo Arqueológico Nacional

The National Archaeology Museum of Spain occupies a huge, Neo-Classical building in the elegant Salamanca neighbourhood, and contains more than 1,300,000 artworks and artifacts that span millennia, and have been gathered from around the world. After an expensive and lengthy renovation, the museum reopened its doors in 2014 with more than 10,000 sq m (12,000 sq yds) of gallery space to show off its dazzling collection. Major attractions include enigmatic female statues, sculpted by Iberian tribes more than 2,000 years ago, glittering collections of Visigothic goldwork and even some curious and unique early calculators.

Tesoro de Guarrazar ①

This magnificent hoard of Visigothic votive crowns and crosses, discovered in a Spanish orchard in the mid-19th century, dates back to the 7th century. One of the finest pieces is the golden votive Crown of Recesvinto, studded with blue sapphires **(right)**.

② Dama de Elche

This is Spain's answer to the Mona Lisa **(left)** – a polychrome bust of a female figure which dates from the 4th century BC. The "Lady of Elche" is remarkable for its sophistication, the superb quality of the carving, and the woman's enigmatic expression.

③ Coin and Medal Collection

The museum's collection of coins and medals is one of the largest and finest in Europe. Among the earliest coins are a Carthaginian Trishekel, and a silver Tetradrachm engraved with the profile of Ptolemy IV, both of which date to the 3rd century BC.

Bote de Zamora ④

This exquisitely carved, ivory urn **(right)** is considered to be one of the greatest jewels of Islamic art, and was commissioned by Al-Hakam II, the Caliph of Cordoba, for Subh, a Basque slave who became his favourite concubine but died young.

⑤ Dama de Baza

Another of the remarkable Iberian statues depicting a female figure, the 4th-century BC Lady of Baza is seated on an armchair **(left)**, and features the same inscrutable expression as her more celebrated neighbour in the same gallery.

⑥ Estela de Solana de Cabañas

Dating back to between 1000 and 800 BC, this Bronze Age engraved stone discovered in Cáceres is thought to be a funerary stela, and depicts a heroic figure surrounded by chariots and weapons **(right)**.

⑦ Puteal de la Moncloa

This large Roman marble well is carved with graceful figures from Greek myths, including the birth of Athena in Olympus. The well was acquired by Felipe V in the 18th century.

⑧ Orante Sumerio

Purchased for the museum's collection in 2007, this elegant praying figure was carved around 2,500 BC in Mesopotamia (now Iraq). Sumerian votive figures like this one were commissioned for temples.

⑨ Husillos Sarcophagus

The museum has an extensive collection of Roman art and statuary. This richly decorated sarcophagus **(below)**, carved in Rome for a wealthy patron and brought to Hispania, depicts the story of Orestes, who figures prominently in several Greek tragedies.

⑩ Ábaco Neperiano

This cabinet of bronze and ivory rods and strips, engraved with multiplication tables **(left)**, is a rare 17th-century calculator. It was invented by John Napier of Edinburgh and is often called "Napier's bones".

NEED TO KNOW

MAP X9 ■ Calle Serrano, 13 ■ Metro Serrano (Line 4) and Retiro (Line 2) ■ Buses 1, 9, 19, 51, 74 ■ 91 577 79 12 ■ www.man.es

Open 9:30am–8pm Tue–Sat, 9:30am–3pm Sun and public hols ■ Adm €3 (free 2–8pm Sat, 9:30am–3pm Sun)

■ Shop; café with terrace; wheelchair-accessible.

■ A free multimedia app featuring an interactive guide (also suitable for the sight- and hearing-impaired) is available from iTunes.

Museum Guide
The main entrance is on Calle Serrano. The collection is laid out chronologically, with the Prehistoric section on the ground floor; Roman, Late Antiquity, Medieval Al-Andalus and Protohistory galleries on the first floor, and the Medieval and Modern Era collections on the second floor. Coins and medals are displayed on a mezzanine level between the first and second floors. The Dama de Elche, the museum's star exhibit, is found in Room 13.

🔟 ⭐ El Escorial

Occupying a majestic setting in the southern foothills of the Sierra de Guadarrama, the Royal Monastery of San Lorenzo de El Escorial was commissioned by Felipe II as a mausoleum for the tomb of his father, Carlos I. The name commemorates the victory over the French at St Quentin on the Feast of St Lawrence in 1557. Building began in 1563 and the king took a keen interest in the smallest details. The complex was completed in 1595 and comprised a basilica, a royal palace, a monastery, a seminary and a library. This monument to the king's personal aspirations, and the ideals of the Counter-Reformation still inspires awe, if not always affection.

1 Basilica
The basilica **(below)** takes the form of a Greek cross, and has vaults decorated with exquisite frescoes by Luca Giordano.

Sierra de Guadarrama and Monasterio de El Escorial

2 King's Apartments
King Felipe II's personal quarters are surprisingly modest – just three simply furnished rooms with white-washed walls and terracotta tiling. Look out for the hand chair that was used to carry the gout-ridden king on his last journey here in 1598.

3 Pantheon of the Kings
Work on the domed burial chamber, situated directly under the high altar of the basilica, was completed in 1654. The walls were surfaced with marble, bronze and jasper by Giovanni Battista Crescenzi.

4 Chapter Houses
The vaulted ceilings were decorated in the 17th century by Italian artists Fabrizio Castello and Nicolas Granelo. Hanging from the walls are priceless canvases by Titian, Tintoretto, Veronese, Velázquez and El Greco.

5 Library
The magnificent barrel-vaulted hall **(below)** has stunning ceiling frescoes by Italian artists. The shelves contain 4,000 precious manuscripts and 40,000 folio volumes – arranged facing outwards to allow air to permeate the pages.

FELIPE II'S VISION

Before architect Juan Bautista de Toledo could start on El Escorial, Felipe gave him precise instructions: "[It should have] simplicity in the construction, severity in the whole, nobility without arrogance, majesty without ostentation." It was designed to resemble the iron grid on which St Lawrence was burned.

6 Main Staircase
Look upwards from this magnificent staircase to admire the "Glory of the Spanish monarchy" frescoes **(above)** by Luca Giordano.

8 Strolling Gallery
Felipe II enjoyed indoor walks in this airy gallery. The meridians on the floor were added in the 18th century.

9 Courtyard of the Kings
This courtyard **(below)** offers the best view of the basilica façade, its twin belltowers and awe-inspiring dome. Look out for the larger-than-life statues over the portal, of Old Testament kings.

7 Gallery of Battles
This gallery is decorated with superb frescoes by 16th-century Italian artists. The paintings were intended to validate Felipe II's military campaigns.

10 Architecture Museum
This small exhibition of plans, scale models and workmen's tools explains how El Escorial was constructed. Note the wooden cranes and hoists used to haul the blocks of granite into place.

NEED TO KNOW

Calle de Juan de Borbón y Battenberg ■ Train C-8 from Atocha or Chamartín to El Escorial, then bus from train station to San Lorenzo de El Escorial; buses 661 & 664 from Moncloa to San Lorenzo El Escorial ■ 91 890 5904 ■ www.patrimonio nacional.es

Open Apr–Sep: 10am–8pm Tue–Sun; Oct–Mar: 10am–6pm Tue–Sun; closed 11 & 12 Nov and public hols

Adm €10, €5 (concessions), €4 + ticket price (for a guided tour) ■ The Bourbon rooms (Aposentos de los Borbones) are currently closed to the public ■ Adm €3.60

■ San Lorenzo de El Escorial has a good selection of bars and restaurants.

■ Queues build up after midday, and on Wed and Thu 5–8pm Apr–Sep and 3–6pm Oct–Mar when admission is free.

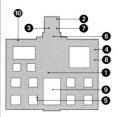

Plan of El Escorial

Further Features of El Escorial

1 Cenotaphs
These superb bronze sculptures on either side of the high altar are by an Italian father and son team, Leone and Pompeo Leoni. On the left is Carlos I (Emperor Charles V), shown with his wife, daughter and sisters; opposite are Felipe II, three of his wives and his son, Don Carlos.

Calvary by Rogier van der Weyden

2 King's Deathbed
In this simple canopied bed, Felipe II died on 13 September 1598, it is said as "the seminary children were singing the dawn mass". The bed was positioned so that the king could easily see the high altar of the basilica on one side and the mountains of the Sierra de Guadarrama on the other.

3 The Martyrdom of St Maurice and the Theban Legion
This ethereal work by El Greco (1541–1614) **(right)** was intended for an altar in the basilica, but Felipe II found the style inappropriate and relegated it to the sacristy. El Greco never received another royal commission.

The Martyrdom of St Maurice

4 Portrait of Felipe II
In this stately painting by Dutch artist Antonio Moro, the king, then aged 37, is wearing the suit of armour he wore at the battle of St Quentin in France in 1557. It was to be Felipe's only victory on the battlefield.

5 Cellini Crucifix
Florentine master craftsman Benvenuto Cellini sculpted this exquisite image of Christ from a single block of Carrara marble. It was presented to Felipe II in 1562 by Francisco de Medici, Grand Duke of Tuscany.

6 Calvary
This moving painting **(left)** is by 15th-century Flemish artist Rogier van der Weyden. Felipe II knew the Netherlands well and was an avid collector of Flemish art.

7 Last Supper
Venetian artist Titian undertook numerous commissions for El Escorial. Unfortunately his *Last Supper* canvas was too big to fit the space assigned to it in the monks' refectory and was literally cut down to size.

8 Inlay Doors
One of the most striking features of the king's apartments is the superb marquetry of the inlay doors. Made by German craftsmen in the 16th century, they were sent as a gift to Felipe II from Emperor Maximilian II.

9 King's Treasures
A cupboard in the royal bedchamber contains more than a dozen priceless *objets d'art*. They include a 12th-century chest made in Limoges and a 16th-century "peace plate" by Spanish craftsman Luís de Castillo.

10 Queen's Room Organ
The corridors of El Escorial would have resounded to monastic plainchant, but organ music also met with royal approval. This hand organ dates from the 16th century and is decorated with Felipe II's coat of arms.

KING FELIPE II

When Felipe II took over the reins of government from his father Carlos I in 1556, he inherited not only the Spanish kingdoms of Castile and Aragon, Naples, Sicily, Milan and the Low Countries, but also the Spanish territories of the New World. Defending this far-flung empire embroiled him in constant warfare.

Felipe II

The drain on the royal coffers (despite the prodigious influx of gold and silver from the Americas) led to unpopular tax increases at home, and eventual bankruptcy. Felipe's enemies, the Protestant Dutch, their English allies and the Huguenot French, set out to blacken his reputation, portraying him as a cold and bloodthirsty tyrant. Today's historians take a more objective view, revealing him to have been a conscientious, if rather remote, ruler, and a model family man with a wry sense of humour. On one occasion he startled the monks of El Escorial by encouraging an Indian elephant to roam the cloisters and invade the monastic cells.

**TOP 10
EL ESCORIAL
STATISTICS**

1 2,673 windows
2 1,200 doors
3 300 monastic cells
4 88 fountains
5 86 stairways
6 73 statues
7 42 chapels (basilica)
8 16 courtyards
9 14 entrance halls
10 80,000 visitors a year

This fine view of the Monastery of El Escorial dates from the 16th century and is in the Biblioteca Nacional in Madrid

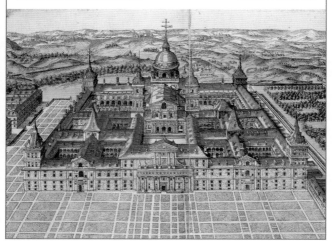

The Top 10 of Everything

Traditional Iberian tin-glazed
ceramic tiles, known as *azulejos*

🔟 Moments in History

Auto-da-fe on Plaza Mayor (1680) by Francisco Rizi, Prado Museum

1 Birth of a City

The first inhabitants of Madrid were Muslim soldiers under the command of Muhammad I. The founding of the city is usually dated to AD 852 when a fortress *(alcázar)* was built on the escarpment now occupied by the Palacio Real *(see pp12–15)*. Few traces of this early settlement survive, apart from a small section of the city wall *(see p112)*.

2 Christian Conquest

Muhammad I had his fortress built to guard against attack from northern Christian armies, and to protect the important city of Toledo. In 1083 Toledo fell and the *alcázar* of Madrid was surrendered without a fight. The new Christian settlers lived harmoniously with their Arab neighbours, but mosques were changed to churches.

3 New Capital

In 1561 Felipe II took the decision to make Madrid his new capital (previously Valladolid had been preferred). The central location and proximity to other royal residences were determining factors. Madrid

Felipe II

was still a small, squalid town of 9,000 inhabitants – one of the king's first decisions was to transform the old marketplace outside the walls into a public square, now Plaza Mayor *(see pp22–3)*.

4 Golden Age

By the time that Plaza Mayor was completed (1619) Madrid's population had swollen to around 85,000. Courtiers, noblemen, clerics and criminals descended on the city, leading to such overcrowding that Felipe IV ordered the building of a new perimeter wall. Madrid provided rich material for the playwrights of the Golden Age, including Lope de Vega and Tirso de Molina.

5 Mayor-King

Madrid thrived during the reign of Carlos III (1759–88). He gave the city magnificent gateways such as the Puerta de Alcalá *(see p82)*, and imposing thoroughfares such as the Paseo del Prado *(see p78–83)*. Streets were paved and lit, sewers were dug and nightwatchmen introduced. He became known as *El Rey-Alcalde* (the Mayor-King).

Moments in History « **47**

6 Insurrection

On 2 May 1808, two months after a French army occupied the city, the people of Madrid rose in revolt. Fierce street battles were fought, while the troops of the Monteleón barracks mutinied in support of the rebels. But within a few hours, the insurrection had been crushed and the leaders were executed by firing squad.

7 Re-Awakening

In 1919 Alfonso XIII opened Madrid's first metro line and the city was – literally – on the move again, after decades of inertia. Whole streets were demolished to make way for the Gran Vía's bars and restaurants, and Calle de Alcalá became the heart of a new financial district.

8 Madrid Under Siege

Three months into the Spanish Civil War, General Franco's Nationalist army surrounded Madrid. Republican resistance was fierce and the siege dragged on for two-and-a-half years, with the city eventually only falling to the rebel forces in March 1939.

General Franco

9 Death of Franco

After ruling Spain with an iron fist for 36 years, General Franco died in November 1975, leaving power in the hands of his designated successor, Prince (later King) Juan Carlos I. The first democratic elections were held in June 1977.

10 Tejero's Coup

On 23 February 1981 Franco loyalists under Colonel Antonio Tejero attempted a coup. Tejero forced his way into the parliament building, firing shots into the air. The conspiracy collapsed when the king confirmed that the army had remained loyal.

TOP 10 FIGURES IN MADRID HISTORY

Joseph Bonaparte

1 Al-Mundhir
According to some historians, Muhammad I's son was the true founder of the city.

2 Isidro Merlo y Quintana
This devout farm labourer inspired miracles after his death in 1172 and became the city's patron saint.

3 Felipe II
When in Madrid, the king stayed in the Alcázar or with the monks of San Jerónimo monastery.

4 Félix Lope de Vega
Spain's greatest playwright was banned from Madrid for eight years after libelling the father of his former lover.

5 Carlos III
Madrid's "best mayor" spent little of the first part of his reign in the city, but his long-term impact is undeniable.

6 Luis Daoíz
With Pedro Velarde, Daoíz led the insurrection against the French in 1808, and died in the fighting.

7 Joseph Bonaparte
Detested during his short reign as King of Spain (1808–13), he did plan one of the city's finest squares, Plaza de Oriente (see p103).

8 Gustavo Durán
One of the most courageous commanders defending Madrid during the Civil War.

9 General Francisco Franco
Statues around the city that once honoured the former dictator have all been removed.

10 Enrique Tierno Galván
Madrid's most popular mayor ran the city from 1979 until his death in 1986, during a time of great cultural change.

🔟 Museums and Galleries

Beautifully ornate Salón Chaflán at the Museo Cerralbo

① Museo Cerralbo

This astonishingly diverse collection – paintings, sculptures, tapestries, glassware, porcelain and more – was originally the property of the 17th Marquis of Cerralbo. The museum's 30,000 artifacts are housed in his palace and the rooms offer a fascinating window onto the life of Spanish aristocracy at the beginning of the 20th century *(see p101)*.

② Museo Nacional del Prado

The world-famous gallery is housed in Juan de Villanueva's Neo-Classical masterpiece – an artistic monument in its own right. The relief above the Velázquez Portal depicts Fernando VII as guardian of the arts and sciences – it was during his reign that the Prado opened as an art gallery. Its strongest collection, unsurprisingly, is its Spanish artworks, particularly those of Francisco Goya *(see pp16–21)*.

③ Museo Thyssen-Bornemisza

The setting for this outstanding collection is the Palacio de Villahermosa, remodelled in the 1990s and with a dramatic new wing added in 2005. Carmen Thyssen-Bornemisza, widow of the preceding baron, was responsible for the salmon-pink colour scheme inside. The museum holds international art from the 14th century onwards *(see pp28–31)*.

④ Museo Nacional Centro de Arte Reina Sofía

This treasure-house of modern Spanish art was designed as a hospital by Francisco Sabatini in 1756. The conversion to art gallery was completed in 1990. The glass lifts offer panoramic views of the city *(see pp32–5)*.

⑤ Museo de América

While the fabled treasures shipped back to Spain by Cortés, Columbus and Pizarro were exhibited as early as 1519, most of the precious items disappeared or were melted down. A great many of the exquisite and fascinating ethnological and ethnographical exhibits on show here originate from Carlos III's "cabinet of natural history", founded in the 18th century, and the museum's displays now embrace the entire American continent *(see p101)*.

Quimbaya gold censer, Museo de América

6 Museo Arqueológico Nacional

Founded by Queen Isabel II in 1867, the archaeological museum contains treasures from most of the world's ancient civilizations, with an emphasis on the Iberian Peninsula. Highlights include the carved sculpture, the "Lady of Elche", a noblewoman from the 4th century BC (see pp38–9 & p84).

7 Real Academia de Bellas Artes de San Fernando

The Academy of Fine Arts was founded by Fernando VI in 1752 and moved into the Goyeneche Palace 25 years later. Among the highlights are works by Spanish artists El Greco, Velázquez, Murillo, Zurbarán and Goya, as well as an array of European masterpieces (see p94).

8 Casa-Museo de Lope de Vega

Spain's greatest playwright Félix Lope de Vega (see p47) lived in this house between 1610 and 1635. Now a museum, its rooms are furnished in the style of the period, based on an inventory by the dramatist himself (see p108).

9 Museo Sorolla

The home of Valencian artist Joaquín Sorolla (1863–1923) is now a museum displaying his work. Sorolla won international recognition after his paintings were shown in the Exposition Universelle in Paris (1901). His canvases are brilliant evocations of Spanish life. One of his best-loved works depicts his wife and daughter on the Valencia seashore (see p87).

Walk on the Beach by Sorolla at Museo Sorolla

10 Museo Nacional de Artes Decorativas

One of the many pluses of the Decorative Arts Museum is that it sets Spanish crafts in a European context. Highlights include a Gothic bedroom, Flemish tapestries and a lovely collection of 19th-century fans (see p81).

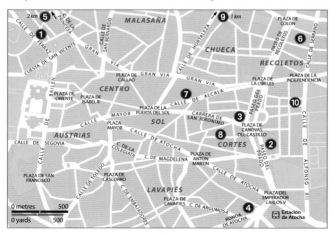

🔟 Architectural Sights

Ceiling of Palacio Real

1 Palacio Real

The Royal Palace marks a decisive break with the austere tastes of Spain's Habsburg rulers. Felipe V had been brought up at Versailles where the International Baroque style was in vogue. Architect Filippo Juvarra died two years into the project, but his successor, Gian Battista Sachetti retained the Baroque spirit *(see pp12–15)*.

2 Plaza Mayor

The inspiration for the square was El Escorial's courtyard *(see pp40–43)*. But the plans of architect Juan de Herrera were realized only 30 years later, in 1619, by Gómez de Mora *(see pp22–3)*.

3 Palacio de Cibeles

MAP F4 ■ Plaza Cibeles 1

Home of the Madrid City Hall since 2007, this extraordinary building was the first major commission of Galician architect Antonio Palacios and his partner, Joaquín Otamendi. The style of this palace (1907–19) has influences ranging from Spanish Plateresque to Art Nouveau. The most striking feature of the interior is the glass-domed roof.

4 Palacio Longoria

Art Nouveau is usually associated with Barcelona rather than with Madrid and, in fact, this superb example is by the Catalan architect José Grases Riera. Bold and original in design, the palace is full of typical Art Nouveau features, such as the florid sculptural detail, sensuous curves and the balustrade *(see p120)*.

5 Círculo de Bellas Artes

The Fine Arts Club dates from the 1920s and is Antonio Palacios' Art Deco masterpiece. The crowning feature is the statue on the roof, representing the goddess Minerva, patroness of the arts. Pay the one-day membership fee and you can take in the other highlights – the staircase, theatre, ballroom and the Salón de Fiestas, with its painted ceiling *(see p94)*.

6 Metrópolis

One of Madrid's signature buildings, Metrópolis was designed in 1905 by the French architects Jules and Raymond Février. The high points – literally – of this lovely Neo-Baroque design are the bronze wreaths garlanding the cupola, which glint in the sunlight *(see p94)*.

Metrópolis

7 Iglesia de San Jerónimo el Real

Though much altered over the years, this 16th-century church is an important architectural monument *(see p82)*. It has also been a place of refuge for Spanish kings and queens through the ages. Former king Juan Carlos I was crowned here in 1975 after the death of General Franco.

8 Puerta de Europa
Plaza de Castilla ▪ Metro Plaza de Castilla

The "Gateway to Europe" is a modern version of a triumphal arch. Twenty-six storeys high, the leaning towers of glass and metal were completed in 1996.

Puerta de Europa

9 Residencia de Estudiantes
Pabellón Transatlántico, Calle del Pinar 21 ▪ Metro Pinar del Rey ▪ Closed to the public

This liberal college was founded in 1910; early alumni here included artist Salvador Dalí and poet Federico García Lorca. Designed by Antonio Flórez, the main building was nicknamed "transatlantic" by students because the balustrade resembled the rail of an ocean liner.

10 Torre Picasso
MAP G1 ▪ Plaza de Pablo Ruíz Picasso, Paseo de la Castellana

The tower's main claim to fame is that, at 157 m (515 ft), it is the tallest building in Madrid. Opened in 1989, it is the work of Japanese architect Minoru Yamasaki, designer of the ill-fated former World Trade Center towers in New York.

TOP 10 PLACES TO SEE AZULEJOS (TILES)

Fatigas del Querer

1 Fatigas del Querer
MAP P4 ▪ Calle de la Cruz 17
The interior of this 1920's tavern is decorated with Andalusian tiles and murals.

2 Taberna la Dolores
Tiled mosaics adorn the façade of this *taberna* dating from 1908 *(see p83)*.

3 Viva Madrid
Tiled inside and out; look for the Cibeles fountain on the façade *(see p115)*.

4 Tablao Villa Rosa
Fantastic ceramic decor dates from the days when this restaurant was a flamenco club *(see p115)*.

5 Antigua Huevería and Farmacia Juansé
MAP D2 ▪ Calle de S Vicente Ferrer
Two tiled frontages. The pharmacy advertised "inoffensive cigarettes", while the painted hens next door provide a clue that this bar was once an egg shop *(huevería)*.

6 Taberna Ángel Sierra
Stunning tiled façade and interior, from the early 20th century *(see p125)*.

7 Taberna Almendro 13
Andalusian decor can be found in this typical tapas bar *(see p116)*.

8 La Fontana de Oro
MAP P4 ▪ Calle de la Victoria 1
Pretty old café converted into a Guinness pub.

9 Restaurante la Quinta del Sordo
MAP C5 ▪ Calle del Sacramento 10
The tiled façade here features scenes from Goya's paintings.

10 Taberna de la Daniela
Ceramic motifs cover the bar and façade of this classic Madrid *taberna (see p90)*.

⓾ Off the Beaten Track

Parque Quinta de los Molinos

① Parque Quinta de los Molinos

MAP B1 ▪ Calle Alcalá 527 ▪ Open 8am–midnight Mon–Fri; 10 am–6pm Sat–Sun ▪ Metro Suanzes

Every spring, hundreds of almond trees blossom in clouds of pink and white in this beautiful little park, which dates back to 1920.

② Hammam Al Ándalus

MAP N5 ▪ C/Atocha, 14, ▪ 91 429 90 20 ▪ Adm ▪ Open 10am–10pm daily ▪ www.madrid.hammamalandalus.com

Recover from museum-fever and tramping the Madrid pavements in this hammam, which has soothing Andalus-style decor, warm baths and a massage service.

③ Museo del Aire (Museo de Aeronáutica y Astronáutica de España)

MAP A2 ▪ Aeródromo de Cuatro Vientos, Ctra de Extremadura, km 10,500 ▪ 91 509 16 90 ▪ Open 10am–2pm Tue–Sun ▪ All buses on the Madrid-Alcorcón-Móstoles route from Príncipe Pío station; Metro Cuatro Vientos, then 1 km walk or bus

Ideal for kids, the Spanish Air Force's museum contains one of the largest collections of vintage aircraft in Europe. On display are helicopters, jet fighters and more, including a Breguet 19 that crossed the Southern Atlantic Ocean in 1929.

④ CentroCentro chill-out lounge

MAP F4 ▪ Plaza Cibeles 1 ▪ 91 480 0008 ▪ www.centrocentro.org

In what was once the main hall of Madrid's opulent former post office (and now city hall), you'll find the CentroCentro chill-out lounge. With brightly coloured sofas and a wide choice of newspapers and maga-zines, it's the ideal spot in which to relax before hitting the nearby Prado.

⑤ Matadero Madrid – Centro de Creación Contemporánea

MAP B2 ▪ Plaza de Legazpi 8 ▪ 91 517 7309 ▪ Open 4–9pm Tue–Fri, 11am–9pm Sat, Sun and public hols ▪ Metro Legazpi; bus 6, 8, 18, 19, 45, 78 and 148 ▪ Free, but adm charge for films and some activities ▪ www.mataderomadrid.org

Located in a beautifully converted former slaughterhouse, this city-run cultural centre is dedicated to the creative output of contemporary artists, and features cutting-edge exhibitions, film screenings at the Cineteca and more. It also has a fantastic café, bar and restaurant.

Real Fábrica de Tapices of Madrid

6 Real Fábrica de Tapices

MAP G6 ■ **Calle de Fuenterrabía, 2** ■ **914 34 05 50** ■ **Metro Menéndez Pelayo or Atocha** ■ **Open 10am–2pm Mon–Fri** ■ **Closed Aug** ■ **Adm by guided visit only (tours every 30 minutes)** ■ **www.realfabricadetapices.com**

Watch exquisite wall-hangings and carpets being made using traditional methods and antique looms at the fascinating Royal Tapestry Factory, which was founded in 1720. It also contains a superb collection of historic textiles created for Spanish monarchs over the centuries.

7 Invernadero de Atocha

MAP F6 ■ **Plaza Emperador Carlos V s/n** ■ **Always open**

On chilly winter days, there's nowhere better to escape from Madrid's biting wind than in this enchanting tropical garden located, bizarrely, in Atocha train station. Luxuriant palm trees reach to the beautiful glass ceiling, while turtles and koi carp swim lazily in the pools below.

8 Museo del Ferrocarril

MAP F6 ■ **Paseo de las Delicias 61** ■ **902 22 88 22** ■ **Metro Delicias** ■ **Open 9:30am–3pm Tue–Fri, 10am–3pm Sat–Sun**

Set in the 19th-century Delicias train station, this wonderful train museum is packed with steam engines, period carriages, model trains and plenty more to amuse the whole family. Even the café is set in a delightful carriage from the 1920s. The museum is also the starting point for the charming Tren de la Fresa (see p82).

9 Andén 0

MAP E1 ■ **Plaza de Chamberí s/n** ■ **902 44 44 03** ■ **Open 9:30am–8:30pm daily**

Madrid has its very own underground "ghost station": the Chamberí metro stop (its new name means "Platform Zero") was closed in 1966 and hasn't changed since, except to fall into disrepair. Now lovingly restored to its former glory, it is a small and fascinating museum, with exhibits which recall its history and use as a bomb shelter during the Civil War.

10 Roof terrace at the Círculo de Bellas Artes

A sumptuous 1920s art club and cultural centre, the Círculo de Bellas Artes has a secret: its wonderful roof terrace, which can be accessed by a glass lift. Once up on the roof, you can enjoy fabulous city-wide views. It is the perfect spot for late-evening cocktails, and there is occasional live music, too. Note that the roof terrace is sometimes closed for private events, so check in advance. Entry also includes admission to the beautiful café (see p50 and p94).

Círculo de Bellas Artes roof terrace

Following pages Invernadero de Atocha

🔟 Parks and Gardens

The Palacio de Cristal exhibition space in the Parque del Retiro

1 Parque del Retiro

In 1767, Carlos III broke with tradition by allowing members of the public into the Retiro, providing they were "washed and suitably dressed". However it was not until the 1860s and the advent of the First Republic that the partitions separating the royal enclosure from the public area were finally torn down for good (see pp36–7).

2 Real Jardín Botánico

The botanical garden is the perfect place in which to recharge your batteries after the exhausting walk around the Prado Museum. The shady paths are lined with statues, and the air is cooled by judiciously placed fountains (see p80).

3 Jardines del Campo del Moro

MAP A4 ■ Open Apr–Sep: 10am–8pm daily; Oct–Mar: 10am–6pm daily ■ Can close for official ceremonies ■ Dis. access

Surprisingly, these gardens in the grounds of the Palacio Real were not laid out until the 19th century. The name, "Moor's field" refers to the Arab general, Ali Ben Youssef, who is said to have camped here while besieging the city after it had fallen to the Christians in 1109. On a fine day, the views of the palace and the Casa de Campo from these gardens are unbeatable (see pp12–15).

Jardines del Campo del Moro

4 Parque del Oeste

MAP B2 ■ Paseo Moret ■ Dis. access ■ Closed to cars at weekends

This lovely park was designed in the early 20th century by Cecilio Rodríguez, head gardener at the Retiro. Apart from the *rosaleda* (rose garden), the main attraction is the Temple of Debod, an ancient monument dating from the 2nd century BC. It was a gift from the

Egyptian government. Cafés abound on Paseo del Pintor Rosales, which is also a terminus of the Teleférico cable car (see p59).

5 Casa de Campo
Paseo Puerta del Angel 1 (bicycles only) ▪ Metro Lago or Casa de Campo

The city's largest green space, and Felipe II's favourite hunting ground, was opened to the public with the overthrow of the monarchy in 1931. Attractively planted with pines, oaks, poplars and many other trees, there are also huge areas of open space, mostly scrub. Amenities include cafés, picnic areas, restaurants, a boating lake, a zoo and the lively Parque de Atracciones amusement park (see p58).

6 Parque Juan Carlos I
Metro Campo de las Naciones ▪ Open Jun–Sep: 7–1am daily; Oct–May: 7am–11pm Sun–Thu, 7am–midnight Fri & Sat ▪ Dis. access

This attractive park lies within the exhibition grounds of the Campo de las Naciones. Highlights include catamaran trips on the river, superb modern sculptures and the largest fountain in Spain, with 300 jets (see p63).

7 Jardines de Sabatini
MAP J2 ▪ Open May–Sep: 9am–10pm daily; Oct–Apr: 9am–9pm daily

These orderly gardens next to the Palacio Real occupy the site of the royal stables. Laid out in the 1930s,

the design was based on original 18th-century plans. A quiet, restful place for a picnic (see pp12–15).

8 Parque de Berlín
Príncipe de Vergara ▪ Metro Concha Espina ▪ Free ▪ Dis. access

When the Berlin Wall came down in 1989, everyone wanted a piece of the action. Set among the fountains at the far end of this park, near the Auditorio Nacional (see p65), are three sections of the wall with original graffiti. Children's play areas and places to eat and drink are nearby.

9 Estación de Atocha
The space beneath the magnificent iron-and-glass canopy at Madrid's central railway station is occupied by a miniature botanical garden, replete with palms and tropical plants (see p53 and p82).

Temple of Bacchus, Parque El Capricho

10 Parque El Capricho
Paseo de la Alamenda de Osuna 25 ▪ Metro El Capricho ▪ Open 9am–6:30pm Sat, Sun & public hols (to 9pm Apr–Sep) ▪ Closed 1 Jan, 25 Dec ▪ Dis. access

These delightful 18th-century gardens once belonged to the palace of the Duke and Duchess of Osuna and were landscaped by Jean-Baptiste Mulot, the gardener at the palace of Versailles, outside Paris. They have been restored to their former glory with tree-lined paths, fountains, a lake and follies.

Formal layout of the Jardines de Sabatini

🔟 Children's Attractions

1 Zoo-Aquarium
Road A-5, exit (salida) 5 Casa de Campo ■ Metro Casa de Campo ■ Opening times vary, consult website: www.zoomadrid.com/calendario ■ Adm (under 3s free)

Madrid's zoo is considered to be one of the best in Europe – within its confines there are more than 6,000 animals from 500 species, including the endangered white tiger. Young children, in particular, will enjoy the koalas. Free-flying birds of prey are the main attraction of the aviary, while sharks and other creatures of the deep lurk in the Aquarium. The Dolphinarium shows are another popular draw.

Giraffe at the Zoo

2 Parque de Atracciones
Casa de Campo ■ Road A-5, exit (salida) Parque de Atracciones ■ Metro Batán ■ Opening times vary, consult website: www.parquedeatracciones.es/horarios ■ Adm (free for children under 100 cm/ 39 inches in height)

This amusement park has more than 40 stomach-churning rides as well as a host of other diversions such as puppet and magic shows, and a virtual reality zone. The rides include Los Rápidos (a chance to try white-water rafting) and Top Spin, which needs no explanation. For the very young there are merry-go-rounds and train and boat rides.

3 Faunia
Avenida de las Comunidades 28 ■ Road A-3, exit (salida) 6 Valdebernardo ■ Metro Valdebernardo ■ Opening times vary, consult website: www.faunia.es/horarios ■ Dis. access ■ Adm (free for children under 100 cm/ 39 inches in height)

Each of the 13 pavilions in this science park has been designed to recreate a different ecosystem with authentic sights, sounds and smells. Visitors can "experience" a tropical storm, journey to the polar regions and observe nocturnal creatures in their natural habitat.

4 Parque Warner
Camino de la Warner, San Martín de la Vega ■ Road A-4, exit (salida) 22 ■ Train C-3A from Atocha ■ Opening times vary, consult website: www.parquewarner.com/calendario ■ Adm (free for children under 100 cm/ 39 inches in height)

This vast site is divided into themed areas: Superheroes is devoted to the fantasy worlds of Gotham City and Metrópolis, and The Wild West recalls Hollywood westerns of the John Wayne era. You can also tour the replicated film sets of the Warner Brothers Studio.

5 Palacio de Hielo
Calle Silvano 77 ■ 91 716 0400 ■ Metro Canillas ■ Open 10am–10pm daily. Shops: 10am–10pm Mon–Sat, noon–10pm Sun & public hols ■ Shops closed 1 & 6 Jan, 1 May, 25 Dec ■ www.palaciodehielo.com ■ Dis. access ■ Adm

Located in the heart of Madrid, Palacio de Hielo is a retail, leisure and entertainment complex with an Olympic-sized (1,800-sq m/ 2,150-sq yd) ice rink. Skates are available for hire and classes can be taken. It has 12 restaurants and cafés, a children's playground, a bowling alley, a 15-screen cinema and a gym.

Aerial ride at Parque de Atracciones

Food court at Centro Comercial Xanadú

6 Centro Comercial Xanadú

Road A-5, exit (salida) 22 Arroyomolinos ▪ Bus 528, 534 or 539 from Príncipe Pío ▪ Shops: open 10am–10pm daily, closed 1 & 6 Jan, 25 Dec; Cinema and Snow Park: open 10am–10pm daily (to 2am Fri–Sun)

This shopping mall and entertainment centre has an indoor ski slope and ski school. Other amenities include cinemas, restaurants, bowling and go-karting.

7 Aquópolis

Carretera Nacional II (15.5km) San Fernando de Henares ▪ Open Jun: 12:30–7pm (from noon Sat & pub hols); Jul & Aug: 12:30–8pm (from noon Sat & pub hols); Sep: noon–7pm ▪ Adm

On offer at Madrid's water park is a range of giant water slides, toboggans, cascades and spirals. There's also a lake, wave pool and toddlers' paddling pool, as well as cafés and restaurants.

8 Tren de la Fresa

MAP F6 ▪ Museo del Ferrocarril: Paseo de las Delicias 61 ▪ Metro Delicias ▪ Departures: 2, 3, 16, 17, 23, 24, 30 & 31 May; 6, 7, 20 & 21 Jun; 19, 20, 26 & 27 Sep; 3, 4, 17, 18 & 25 Oct: 10am; Return: 6pm ▪ Adm (under 4s free)

Great fun for the kids and a nostalgic journey into the past for the grown-ups, the "Strawberry Train", pulled by an old steam locomotive, follows the original route from Madrid to Aranjuez, which first opened in 1850. Hostesses wearing period costume give out helpings of the strawberries for which Aranjuez is famous. The price of the ticket includes the bus ride from the station, as well as entry to the palace, gardens and other family-friendly attractions.

9 Teleférico

MAP A2 ▪ Paseo del Pintor Rosales ▪ Opening times vary, consult website: www.teleferico.com ▪ Adm (under 3s free)

The cable car ride between Parque del Oeste and Casa de Campo is enjoyable for both kids and parents. There are fabulous views of the city skyline – the leaflet inside the cable car will help you to locate landmarks such as the Telefónica building, Torre Picasso and the Palacio Real.

The Teleférico across Casa de Campo

10 Parque del Retiro

The Retiro's central location makes it an obvious place to visit if the children are in the mood to run wild. At weekends (times vary), take them to the puppet show in the open-air theatre near the lake. They won't need to know any Spanish as the sense of fun is infectious (see pp36–7).

Engine of the Tren de la Fresa

ⓔ Sporting Venues

The impressive exterior of the Estadio Santiago Bernabéu

① Estadio Santiago Bernabéu

Avenida de Concha Espina 1 ■ Metro Santiago Bernabéu ■ Trophy room: Open daily except 1 Jan, 25 Dec ■ Adm (under 5s free)

The venerated Real Madrid football club celebrated its centenary in 2002, although this 81,044-seater stadium was not completed until 1946. It is named after Santiago Bernabéu, the club president who brought the team five successive European championships in the 1950s. This success has continued – in 1998 FIFA, football's world governing body, voted Real Madrid the "best club in the history of football". Its tally to date includes 59 domestic and 15 international trophies, and more than five European and 10 UEFA Champions League cups. Visitors can tour the *sala de trofeos* (trophy room). The club also has its own website and television station, broadcasting 20 hours a day. The players are known locally as *merengues* ("meringues") because of their all-white strip.

② Estadio Vicente Calderón

Paseo de la Virgen del Puerto 67 ■ Metro Pirámides

Real Madrid's arch-rivals, Atlético de Madrid, play across the River Manzanares in a 55,000-seat stadium, completed in 1966. For most of its history, the club has lived in the shadow of Real Madrid, but all is forgotten when the two clash in annual matches, billed as the "dual of the gods". The club's best season was in 1996 when it won a league and cup double, but four years later the club suffered the humiliation of being relegated to the second division. King Felipe VI has been the Honorary President since 2003. In 2016 the club is due to move to a renovated stadium, Estadio La Peineta in San Blas, with seating for 70,000.

③ Palacio de los Deportes

Avenida Filipe II ■ Metro Goya, O'Donnell

Inaugurated in February 2005, the Palacio de los Deportes (Sports Palace) occupies the site of a former sports centre that was destroyed by fire in 2001. The building seats 18,000 spectators and was designed to accommodate several sports including athletics, basketball, handball, tennis and boxing. As well as improving both safety and security measures, the centre's acoustics were enhanced in order to make it a suitable venue for pop and rock concerts.

4 Plaza de Toros
Calle de Alcalá 237 ■ Metro Ventas

Bullfighting enthusiasts are divided as to whether it is a sport or an art form. *Corridas* (fights) take place in the Las Ventas stadium (capacity 24,000), which opened in 1931 and even has its own chapel and hospital. Officially the season runs from March to December, but the real action begins in May with the Feria de San Isidro (see p74).

Plaza de Toros

5 Jogging Venues
Running isn't much fun in Madrid because of the heavy traffic, although an exception is Paseo Pintor Rosales with views of the Parque del Oeste. Most *madrileños* head for the Retiro, Jardines Sabatini, Casa de Campo or Madrid Rio.

6 Outdoor Swimming Pools
Piscina Canal de Isabel II, Avenida de Filipinas 54 ■ Metro Canal

Madrid's outdoor swimming pools are open from June to mid-September. There are three pools in the Casa de Campo (children's, intermediate and Olympic), but they are crowded at weekends. An alternative is the Piscina Canal de Isabel II.

7 Hipódromo de la Zarzuela
Avenida Padre Huidobro, Road A-6, exit (salida) 8 ■ 91 740 0540 ■ Opening times vary, see website: www.hipo dromodelazarzuela.es ■ Closed Dec–Mar ■ Adm Under 18s free

Tickets for horse racing can be booked in advance online by phone or in person at the racetrack on Sundays, 11:30am–3pm. Visit the stables before racing begins to pick the favourite.

8 Madrid Caja Mágica
Parque Lineal del Manzanares, Camino de Perales 23 ■ Opening hours vary according to events being held there

This hi-tech sports complex, designed by architect Dominique Perrault, is dedicated to tennis. It includes 11 indoor and 16 outdoor tennis courts. The site is located close to the Manzanares River, south of the city.

9 Circuito del Jarama
Circuito del Jarama, Road A-1, 28km ■ Bus No. 166 from Plaza Castilla

Fans of motor racing (automovilísmo) or motorcycle racing (motociclísmo) should head to this 100-acre track, near San Sebastián de los Reyes, 28 km (17 miles) northeast of Madrid. Race meetings are held here throughout the summer, though the circuit is undergoing renovation until 2021.

10 Club de Campo Villa de Madrid
Carretera de Castilla 2km ■ Bus Nos. 160, 161 from Moncloa

Golf is big business in Spain, thanks to the interest generated by the likes of champions José Maria Olazábal and the late Severiano Ballesteros. Surprisingly, given the mostly barren terrain, there are several 18-hole courses in the Greater Madrid area. The Club de Campo was designed by Javier Arana in 1957 and is reckoned to be one of the best in Europe.

Club de Campo Villa de Madrid

🔟 Madrid for Free

Madrid Río waterside park on the banks of the Manzanares River

1 Madrid Río

www.esmadrid.com/informacion-turistica/madrid-rio/

This contemporary park near the Puente de Segovia follows the banks of the Manzanares River, and offers gardens, children's play areas, bicycle and jogging paths, as well as viewing points, fountains and bridges. There's also a skate park, a climbing wall and facilities for playing basketball, pétanque and paddle tennis. In summer it even boasts its own beach, which attracts Madrileños in droves.

2 Paseo del Arte Museums

Madrid's trio of world-class museums all offer free entry at specific times. The Prado (see pp16–21) is free Mondays to Saturdays from 6–8pm and on Sundays from 5–7pm. The Museo Thyssen-Bornemisza (see pp28–31) is free on Mondays from noon to 4pm, and the Museo Nacional Centro de Arte Reina Sofía (see pp32–5) is free Mondays to Saturdays from 7–9pm and on Sundays from 1:30–7pm.

Entrance to Centro Cultural Conde Duque

3 Local Festivals

The biggest festival in Madrid is held in honour of the city's patron saint, San Isidro, and takes place for a week around 15 May. Local people, dressed in traditional costume, head to the Parque de San Isidro to enjoy outdoor concerts, picnics, and the stalls selling a wide range of food and drink that line the streets. There are plenty of traditional festivals throughout the year, including the Fiestas del Dos de Mayo, held for a week around 2 May in Malasaña, and the Verbena la Paloma which takes place in La Latina in August.

4 Centro Cultural Conde Duque

This huge, city-run cultural centre is home to Madrid's Contemporary Art Museum, and also features an auditorium, a library and several exhibition spaces. All exhibitions, including those in the Contemporary Art Museum, are free, and there is a regular programme of talks, workshops and kid-friendly activities on offer (see p64 and p121).

5 La Casa Encendida

MAP E6 ▪ Ronda de Valencia 2 ▪ 902 43 03 22 ▪ Open 10am–10pm Tue–Sun ▪ www.lacasaencendida.es

This fantastic cultural centre, run by a private foundation, offers a wide range of free exhibitions, workshops, courses and family-friendly activities, and has a charming rooftop garden with fabulous views over the city.

6 Observatorio Astronómico

Madrid's charming 19th-century observatory is free to visit, although by appointment only. Visitors can admire the handsome late 18th-century interior, and a fine collection of historic telescopes (see p82).

7 Palacio de Cristal

The magnificent glass palace (see p37) in the Parque del Retiro has been converted into one of Madrid's most beautiful galleries, and it hosts temporary exhibitions run by the Museo Nacional Centro de Arte Reina Sofía (see pp32–5). Due to the palace's unusual construction, there are no visits on rainy days.

8 Parque Juan Carlos I

This enormous park is where *Madrileños* come to stroll, cycle (free bicycles are available by the hour) and to enjoy a picnic. There are play areas for kids, plenty of free, family-friendly activities at weekends and there is even a little train that will take you around the park (see p57).

Parque Juan Carlos I

9 Planetario de Madrid

Parque Tierno Galván, Av del Planetario 16 ▪ 914 67 34 61 ▪ Metro Mendez Alvaro ▪ Opening hours vary, consult website: www.planetmad.es
While the planetarium's projection shows charge admission, you can visit the exhibition galleries, which have fascinating interactive and audio-visual exhibits, for free.

10 Municipal Museums

Many offer free admission, such as the Museo de Arte Público.

TOP 10 MONEY-SAVING TIPS

Madrid Metro sign

1 Fill up with a *menú del día* (set-price lunch) or *plato combinado* (dish of the day) on weekday lunchtimes for around €10.

2 The Bono Metrobus pass allows you to make 10 metro or bus journeys for €12.20.

3 An Abono Turístico travel pass is ideal if you are using public transport extensively: valid for 1–7 days, it costs from €8.40.

4 Get 20 per cent off admission and go straight to the front of the queue with the Paseo del Arte card, which provides entry to the Prado, Thyssen and Reina Sofía Museums for €25.60.

5 Buy your picnic supplies from one of the city's fantastic markets and head to a park for an alfresco lunch.

6 Check out Atrápalo for discounted entrance tickets to popular concerts, shows and sports events in Madrid. **www.atrapalo.com (Spanish only)**

7 Many theatres and cinemas offer reduced ticket prices on the Día del Espectador (Viewer's Day) each week, usually a Monday, Tuesday or Wednesday.

8 Some of Madrid's bars continue the fine old tradition of providing free *tapas* with your drinks: these include El Tigre (Calle Infantas 30, Chueca), and La Pequeña Graná (C/Embajadores 124, Embajadores).

9 Shoes and other leatherware bargains can be found in the outlets on and around the Calle Augusto Figueroa in Chueca.

10 Hotel breakfasts across Spain are generally pricey and poor value: you'll eat much better elsewhere for less.

Entertainment Venues

① Centro Cultural Conde Duque

MAP C2 ■ **Calle del Conde Duque 11** ■ **www.condeduquemadrid.es**

For most of the year this cultural centre hosts temporary art exhibitions. During the annual Summer Arts Festival, opera, plays and concerts are also on the programme, with many of the events staged outdoors *(see pp74–5)*.

② Cine Doré

MAP E5 ■ **Calle de Santa Isabel 3**

This beautiful 1920s cinema is now the headquarters of the Spanish National Film Institute. There are two screens showing an excellent selection of classic and contemporary films in the original version, and at very reasonable prices. During the summer, films are also shown on an outdoor screen on the terrace (book ahead). The café in the foyer is a good place to meet up with friends *(see p112)*.

③ Teatro Real

MAP C4 ■ **Plaza de Isabel II**

Since its renovation in the 1990s, Madrid's splendid opera house has gone from strength to strength. This is the venue for classical operas, such as works by Mozart and Verdi, performed by international and Spanish companies. The season runs from September to July. If all you want to do is look around, the theatre is open for tours and there's a café in the former ballroom *(see p102)*.

④ Teatro Nacional de la Zarzuela

MAP E4 ■ **Calle de Jovellanos 4** ■ **91 524 5400**

This beautiful theatre dates from 1856 and was built especially to stage *zarzuela*, a form of light opera unique to Spain, and especially popular in Madrid. After decades of neglect, *zarzuela* is now being revived and the theatre commissions new works from time to time, as well as performing classic farces such as *The Barber of Lavapiés* and *The Pharoah's Court*. The season runs from September to June. During the summer, the theatre is used for flamenco, ballet and a range of other cultural events.

⑤ Teatro Fernán Gómez

MAP G2 ■ **Plaza de Colón 4** ■ **91 436 2540**

Events at this important arts centre range from temporary art exhibitions to ballet, jazz, dramatic plays, *zarzuela* and experimental theatre.

Elegant façade of the Teatro Real

Casa de América

6 Casa de América
MAP F3 ■ Plaza de Cibeles s/n

The Neo-Baroque Palacio de Linares, an architectural monument in its own right, dominating the southern end of the Paseo de Recoletos, is now a cultural centre showcasing Latin American arts. It offers a regular programme of films, exhibitions and concerts. There is also a good bookshop, a café and the Cien Llaves restaurant.

7 Fundación Juan March
MAP H1 ■ Castelló 77

Fans of modern art will enjoy the temporary exhibitions held here, which are of world-class standard. The cultural and scientific foundation also sponsors lunchtime chamber concerts and recitals on weekdays, usually starting around noon (the monthly programme is available from the centre). While you are here, take a look at some of the modern sculptures in the forecourt such as *Meeting Place* (1975) by Eduardo Chillida *(see p86)*.

8 Sala la Riviera
MAP A4 ■ Paseo Bajo de la Virgen del Puerto ■ Metro Puerta del Angel, Príncipe Pío

If you're interested in hearing pop and rock acts such as Nickelback, Noel Gallagher or The Vaccines, this is where they're most likely to perform while in Madrid. Acoustics and visibility are both good (better than many venues) and fans can cool off in the summer when the roof is drawn back. It is also a lively and popular club, featuring top local and international DJs.

9 Teatro Monumental
MAP E5 ■ Calle de Atocha 65

Designed by Teodoro Anasagasti in 1922, this theatre, renowned for its acoustics, is the home of both the RTVE orchestra and choir (Spain's state radio and television company), as well as the acclaimed Madrid Symphony Orchestra.

10 Auditorio Nacional de Música
Calle del Príncipe de Vergara 146 ■ Metro Prosperidad, Cruz del Rayo

This modern concert hall, in a residential district north of the centre, is the home of the National Orchestra of Spain, and the major venue for symphony concerts from October to June. The Orchestra of the Comunidad de Madrid also performs here, as do a number of international ensembles.

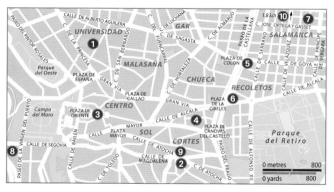

🔟 Bars

Photographs of celebrity customers on the wall at Museo Chicote

① Museo Chicote

In the 1930s, "the best bar in Spain" was Ernest Hemingway's verdict on this cocktail bar. It was in the 1950s and 1960s, however, that Chicote became really famous, thanks to visiting Hollywood celebrities such as Frank Sinatra. The bar is at its best in the late evening *(see p98)*.

② La Ardosa

This popular watering hole has a pedigree going back more than 200 years – Goya sold some of his paintings here. The pub was given a makeover in the 1980s and the owner claims it was the first bar in Madrid to celebrate St Patrick's night. That was when they started serving Guinness and home-made *tortilla*, one of the mainstays of an enticing *tapas* menu. The subdued lighting, mellow music and amiable clientele create a positively addictive ambience *(see p125)*.

③ Café Manuela

"Manuela" as in Manuela Malasaña *(see p120)*. The statue of the local heroine is a feature of the lovely late 19th-century decor, which includes mirrors, fluted columns and stucco flourishes. The entertainment ranges from concerts and poetry readings (sometimes bilingual) to discussions and exhibitions by local artists. The friendly staff serves coffee, beer, cocktails and *tapas (see p124)* depending on the time of day.

④ Ramses

Swing by the Puerta de Alcalá at 1am and spot Ferraris double parked outside this Philippe Starck-designed complex. Popular with Madrid's most fashionable crowd, the large, oval cocktail bar is perfect for people-watching, where an extensive selection of drinks is served. There are also two great restaurants and a club in the basement. The delicious weekend brunch is a good hangover cure; choose a table with a view of the plaza (see p90).

5 Sala Clamores

Once a classic jazz café, this bar is now one of the best-known places in Madrid to enjoy live music. Listen to jazz, blues, funk, or tango performances by renowned artists while sipping cocktails at this large, yet intimate club.

6 Cervecería Santa Bárbara

A Madrid institution, this large beer hall is the perfect place to unwind after a day's sightseeing, or to begin a night on the town. Both dark beer and lager are available on draught – some *Madrileños* like to mix the two (see p125).

7 Cervecería Alemana

This beer and *tapas* bar owes a good deal of its popularity to its terrace on Plaza Santa Ana. Like Museo Chicote, the Alemana was a favourite of Ernest Hemingway and other expats. It serves both Spanish and imported beers (see p112).

8 La Venencia

A bar for sherry drinkers who know their fino from their manzanilla, La Venencia opened its doors in 1929 and still does a roaring trade, especially in the evenings when tourists mingle with a loyal local following. The decor is ageing as graciously as the sherries behind the

counter, and there is a good selection of canapés and *tapas* such as *mojama* (flakes of salty dried tuna). It is as forbidden to tip, as it is to spit on the floor (see p116). Note that the bar serves sherry only.

Guests sitting at the bar at Alhambra

9 Alhambra

Designed to look like a bar from the early 1900s with lovely Moorish touches, Alhambra is one of the best places to start the evening if you're about to embark on a tour of the night spots of Sol and Santa Ana. Check out the Andalusian *tapas*, especially the cured meats and spicy sausage. As well as beer and sangria, there's also a good selection of Spanish wine available (see p116).

10 The Roof

With stylish sofas and custom-designed hanging lights, this rooftop terrace and bar has some of the most outstanding views of the city, plus great cocktails and a good selection of music. A quieter lounge can be found inside, along with a VIP bar that is frequented by glamorous celebrities (see p116).

Stunning views from The Roof

🔟 Tapas Bars

1 Tasca La Farmacia

Like all genuine Madrid *tascas*, this pub on the edge of Salamanca serves its customers a tasty appetizer with each drink, to give them an idea of what's on offer. *Croquetas de Bacalao* – béchamel paste deep-fried with nuggets of cod – are the house speciality *(see p90)*.

Casa Ciriaco

2 Casa Ciriaco

When Ciriaco first opened its doors in 1906, most of the customers were artists, writers and other such Bohemian types. Nowadays it's more conventional but Ciriaco has preserved its reputation for excellent *tapas*. The *boquerones* (anchovies in vinegar) go down a treat with a glass of the house wine.

3 Venta El Buscón

Calle Victoria 5 ■ 91 522 54 12
■ Open daily

A traditional *tapas* bar, decorated with artisan tiles and paintings of the Spanish poet Quevedo. It serves typical *tapas madrileñas* at excellent prices, along with a variety of fish and meat dishes. Don't miss the Spanish omelette or the fried squid *(see p116)*.

4 Los Gatos

MAP E5 ■ Calle de Jesús 2
■ 91 429 3067

Bring your camera when you visit this wonderfully over-the-top bar, often overlooked by tourists. Every inch of space is crammed with bric-a-brac – signed basketball shirts, old telephones, beer barrels, bulls' heads and countless other curiosities. Steer your way to the bar for a glass of beer and a plate of shrimps. While you are there, take a look at the tempting array of canapés, filled rolls and delicious *tapas*.

5 Taberna de Antonio Sanchez

This Lavapiés hostelry dates from 1830. The wooden furniture and bullfighting memorabilia are as authentic as the menu of tortilla and stews *(see p117)*.

Taberna de Antonio Sanchez

6 La Casa del Abuelo

Near Plaza Santa Ana, "Grandad's place" is a spit-and-sawdust bar with bags of atmosphere. It's customary to order the house wine to accompany the *tapas* – variations around the humble shrimp. Try them grilled in their shells *(a la plancha)* or peeled and sautéed in oil and garlic *(al ajillo)*. Standing room only *(see p117)*.

7 El Bocaito

The *bocaitos* are small squares of toasted bread, served with a topping of salmon or anchovies. They are the mainstay of an extensive *tapas* menu. Expect quality rather than quantity and keep an eye on how much you're spending, as it's quite easy to run up a fair-sized bill *(see p125)*.

Salmon *tapas*, El Bocaito

8 Bodegas Rosell

Manolo Rosell, the owner of this high-ceilinged *tapas* tavern, has won Spain's "Golden Nose" award for wine-tasting, and proudly serves his discoveries alongside tasty *tapas*. His helpful waiting staff are able to suggest perfect pairings *(see p83)*.

9 El Rincón de Goya

Located just off Calle Goya, this is the perfect place to stop and refuel after shopping in Salamanca. The *tapas* are listed on the wall behind the bar, and the most popular are the large, toasted canapés with toppings such as brie, steak, wild mushrooms and prawns. There is a small seating area by the bar, as well as the cellar bodega, and it's a popular place with locals *(see p90)*.

10 Casa Labra

The specialities here are cod and cod croquettes. If you don't fancy standing at the bar, classic Madrid dishes are served in the gorgeous 19th-century, wood-panelled room at the back *(see p98)*.

TOP 10 TAPAS DISHES

Croquetas

1 Potato dishes
These include *patatas bravas* (fried, with a spicy tomato sauce) or *patatas alioli* (boiled, with a mayonnaise and garlic dressing).

2 Canapés
The toppings for canapés range from anchovies and egg slices to *morcilla* (black pudding) and smoked salmon.

3 Tortilla
The famous Spanish omelette is far thicker than those of other cuisines and is made with sliced potatoes and onions.

4 Pimientos
Peppers are usually served *rellenos* (stuffed with meat, cod or tuna) or *pimientos de padrón* – grilled and salted.

5 Empanadillas
These are small pastries usually with tuna and tomato or meat fillings.

6 Croquetas
Spanish croquettes are made with a thick béchamel sauce and chopped ham, chicken or cod, then deep-fried.

7 Raciones
Larger dishes to share, including hot stews, *jamón Serrano* (cured ham), *chorizo* (spicy sausage) or *queso manchego* (sheep's milk cheese).

8 Conservas
Canned fish, including *boquerones* (anchovies), *mejillones* (mussels) and *berberechos* (cockles).

9 Soldaditos de Pavía
These are cod fingers fried in batter.

10 Gambas
Shrimps are grilled in their shells *(a la plancha)* or peeled and then fried in oil and garlic *(al ajillo)*.

TOP 10 Restaurants

Historic interior of Botín

1 Botín

According to the *Guinness World Records*, Botín is the world's oldest restaurant, having opened its doors in 1725. The dining rooms retain much of their original decor including *azulejos* (tiles) and oak beams, and the atmosphere is convivial. Botín is famous for Castilian fare and the house speciality, roast suckling pig *(see p117)*.

2 DiverXO

Calle de Padre Damián 23 ■ **91 570 0766** ■ **Metro Cuzco** ■ **Open Tue–Sat** ■ **€€€**

Chef David Muñoz, who trained at London's Hakkasan and Nobu, was awarded a third Michelin star in 2013 for his exceptional Spanish–Asian fusion cuisine at DiverXO. There are three tasting menus. The restaurant seats only 30 people so booking is essential. However, reservations cannot be made more than 30 days in advance.

3 Santceloni

MAP G1 ■ **Hotel Hesperia, Paseo de la Castellana 57** ■ **91 210 8840** ■ **Closed Sat L, Sun, public hols, Aug, Easter** ■ **€€€**

This sleek former outpost of the late Catalan chef Santi Santamaria is one of the city's finest restaurants. The menu features superbly prepared, imaginative dishes, such as white prawn with eucalyptus and apple. Booking is essential.

4 Lhardy

Another Madrid institution, founded in 1839, Lhardy's upstairs dining rooms are wonderfully intimate and more than a touch elegant with *belle époque* gilded mirrors, wainscoting, Limoges china and Bohemian crystal. The cooking is *madrileño* rather than French, the house speciality being *cocido* (chickpea stew) *(see p99)*.

5 Casa Lucio

A family restaurant with more than 40 years of history, Casa Lucio is located in the premises of Mesón El Segoviano, where chef Lucio Blázquez began work at the age of 12. Enjoy traditional Spanish dishes made with the best local ingredients – try the delicious stews *(see p116)*.

6 Viridiana

Named after the Buñuel film, this cosy modern *locale* is located between Paseo del Prado and Retiro Park, and is the life's work of its inspired and inspiring chef, Abraham García. This is the perfect restaurant for a special occasion: the menu is imaginative, the dishes are exquisitely presented and the wine list is superb *(see p83)*.

7 Restaurante La Trainera

Named after the long row boats in the Bay of Biscay, where the restaurant has a fishing vessel, Restaurante La Trainera has expanded into a labyrinth of rooms with pine tables and chairs. The menu uses a variety of seafood, not only from the Bay of Biscay but also from Cádiz and the Mediterranean. Try the shellfish salad, *salpicón de mariscos*, and the grilled fish *(see p91)*.

8 Estado Puro

Savour award-winning gastronomic *tapas* at this funky informal establishment run by famed Spanish chef, Paco Roncero. The menu incorporates molecular gastronomy and fusion cuisine to create a medley of sublime flavours and an array of small dishes to mix and match. Try the delicious asparagus tempura *(see p98)*.

Estado Puro

9 Ramón Freixa Madrid

Imaginative chef Ramón Freixa blends tradition with innovation in his two-star Michelin restaurant. On offer are three fabulous tasting menus that include everything from turtle dove sausage to stewed snails, as well as a breathtaking à la carte selection *(see p91)*.

10 Asador Arizmendi

What *Madrileños* prize here is succulent meat and fish, cooked in the traditional manner over charcoal. If you still have room, try the rice pudding *(arroz con leche) (see p117)*.

TOP 10 SPANISH DISHES

1 Cocido Madrileño
This classic Madrid stew might include pigs' trotters, beef shank, chicken, sausage, chickpeas and vegetables.

2 Cochinillo Asado
The Castilian countryside is famous for its suckling pig, slow-roasted in a wood-fired oven until the flesh is tender and the skin is crispy.

3 Callos a la Madrileña
Tripe may not be to everyone's taste, but try it "Madrid-style", with *chorizo*, tomatoes, onions and paprika, and you may change your mind.

4 Bacalao
There are many ways of cooking salted cod. Ernest Hemingway relished *bacalao al ajoarriero*, a cod stew made with tomatoes, peppers and garlic.

5 Paella
The most famous Spanish rice dish is traditionally cooked with seafood, though you'll also find meat-based *paellas* (usually rabbit or chicken).

6 Pulpo a la Gallega
Octopus "Galician style" comes in slices on a layer of potato, with a large dose of oil and a sprinkling of paprika.

7 Fabada Asturiana
This bean soup is served piping hot with *morcilla* (black pudding).

8 Txangurro
Spider crab is a Basque delicacy served mixed with other seafood in its shell.

9 Merluza Rebozada
Another north country favourite is hake fried in breadcrumbs.

10 Gazpacho
Hailing from Andalucia, this famous cold soup's main ingredients are tomatoes, garlic, cucumber and vinegar, with puréed bread for body.

Paella

For a key to restaurant price ranges see p83

🔟 Shops with a Spanish Theme

① Patrimonio Comunal Olivarero

Spain is the largest producer of olive oil in the world and this representative of a grower's cooperative knows his business. As with wines, it is possible to distinguish different varieties of oils by colour, flavour and smell, and tastings here are part of the fun (see p123).

② Capas Seseña
MAP P4 ■ Calle de la Cruz 23

This firm near Sol has been making traditional full-length Spanish capes (capas) since 1901, hand-tailored from the finest wool. Famous clients over the years have included Picasso, Rudolph Valentino, Hillary Clinton, Bruce Springsteen and Michael Jackson. Needless to say, a made-to-measure cape of this quality does not come cheap.

Exterior of the Capas Seseña cape shop

③ Mesquida Restauraciones
MAP J4 ■ Calle Velázquez 156

Religion still plays an important role in Spanish life, and Madrid is famous for shops specializing in devotional objects. Founded more than 40 years ago, this family business furnishes churches and monasteries as far afield as Ireland and Argentina, and has made items for the Pope's summer residence. The shop is a showcase of rosaries, statues, paintings, icons and communion cups.

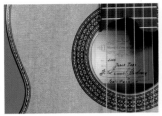

Manuel González Contreras guitar

④ Guitarrar Manuel Contreras

One of Spain's most respected guitar workshops was founded in 1962. Clients have ranged from the classical virtuoso Andrés Segovia to pop guitarist Mark Knopfler. There's a small museum of instruments dating back to the 19th century, and it's fascinating to see the craftsmen at work (see p104).

⑤ Antigua Casa Talavera

Dating back to the early 20th century, Antigua Casa Talavera sells ceramics that are handmade by Spanish potters. Regional styles are represented from all the major centres of ceramics production in Spain, including the famous blue and yellow designs from Talavera de la Reina. Items include decorative tiles, plates, vases, sangria pitchers and reproductions of museum pieces (see p104).

⑥ El Flamenco Vive
MAP L4 ■ Calle Conde de Lemos 7

If you've been won over by flamenco during your stay, now is your chance to look the part. This specialist store has everything – colourful costumes and accessories such as fans,

El Flamenco Vive

flowers and ornamental combs, as well as guitars, books, sheet music, videos, records and CDs (see p104).

7 Terramundi
MAP R5 ■ **Calle Lope de Vega 32**

This Galician restaurant also sells regional produce: *chorizo*, *tetilla* (cream cheese), fish soups, pear compote, strawberry liqueur and wines from the Rias Baixas region.

8 Casa Mira
MAP P4 ■ **Carrera de San Jerónimo 30**

This old-fashioned shop has been producing its famous nougat (*turrón*) for more than 150 years. Made without artificial colourings or preservatives, it's the genuine article.

Bodega Santa Cecilia

9 Bodega Santa Cecilia
MAP C1 ■ **Calle Blasco de Garay 74**

This wine cellar is popular not only for its range (more than 4,000 labels), but also for its quality and affordability. The owners keep prices down by scouring the countryside for lesser-known vineyards.

10 Cuenllas
MAP B2 ■ **Calle Ferraz 5**

This delicatessen is the place for top-quality cured meats and cheeses. Spanish cheeses include Queso Manchego, made from sheep's milk, and the blue cheese, Cabrales. For the finest cured hams, buy *jamón Ibérico* or *Pata Negra* – a breed of pigs fed only on acorns.

TOP 10 MARKETS

Mercado de Sellos

1 El Rastro
Madrid's famous flea market takes place every Sunday morning (see pp26–7).

2 Ferias de Artesanía
Craft fairs spring up all over the city the week before Christmas. Try Plaza Mayor (see pp22–3).

3 Mercado de Sellos
Stamp and coin collectors meet on Sunday mornings under the arches of Plaza Mayor.

4 Mercado de la Cebada
MAP L6 ■ **Plaza de la Cebada s/n** ■ **Mon–Fri & Sat am**
This food market's origins date back to the 16th century (see p114).

5 Mercado de Maravillas
Calle Bravo Murillo 122 ■ **Metro Alvarado** ■ **Mon–Fri & Sat am**
Fresh fruit and vegetables, bread, cured ham and cheese.

6 Mercado de Chamartín
Calle Bolivia 9 ■ **Metro Colombia** ■ **Mon–Fri** (closed at midday) **& Sat am**
Fish and gourmet products.

7 Mercado de San Miguel
Delicatessen stalls selling food and drink to enjoy on site (see p105).

8 Mercado de la Paz
MAP G2 ■ **Calle Ayala 28** ■ **Mon–Fri** (closed at midday) **& Sat am**
The main attraction of this small market is the cheese stalls.

9 Mercado de San Antón
MAP R2 ■ **Calle Augusto Figueroa 24** ■ **Mon–Fri** (closed at midday) **& Sat am**
Flowers, food and wine.

10 Feria del Libro
MAP F6 ■ **Calle de Claudio Moyano** ■ **Mon–Fri** (closed at midday); **Sat & Sun am**
Old, new and second-hand books.

Religious and Cultural Festivals

1 New Year's Eve
31 Dec

To be among the crowds in the Puerta del Sol on the most exciting night of the year is an unforgettable experience. On the stroke of midnight join the revellers in observing the custom of swallowing grapes, one after each chime. Bags of grapes and bottles of sparkling wine are sold from nearby stalls.

2 Epiphany
5 Jan

Rounding off the Christmas festivities is the *Cabalgata de Reyes* (Procession of the Kings). Floats parade along Calle Alcalá, through Puerta del Sol, ending in Plaza Mayor. The three wise men are played by local politicians.

Lively Procession of the Kings

3 Carnival
Feb

The fun begins the weekend before Shrove Tuesday with fancy dress competitions, brass bands and a procession followed by a spectacular show on Plaza Mayor. Ash Wednesday is marked by the "Burial of the Sardine". The mock funeral procession leaves from the church of San Antonio de la Florida and ends with the burial in the Casa de Campo.

Carnival reveller

Penitents carrying the image of Jesus on Holy Thursday

4 Holy Week
Mar/Apr

The three days leading up to Easter are marked by solemn religious processions. On Holy Thursday the image of Jesus is carried through the city by penitents wearing traditional purple hoods, and chains around their feet. The following evening is the procession of Jesús de Medinacelli, which leaves from the basilica of the same name before winding its way around the city centre.

5 San Isidro
15 May

The feast day of Madrid's patron saint is celebrated with a procession to the Ermita de San Isidro, to the south-west of the city. *Madrileños* dress up in traditional costumes and picnic on *rosquillas* (doughnuts). There is also a fair, brass bands and sports events. San Isidro also marks the beginning of the bullfighting season.

6 Veranos de la Villa
Jul–Sep

The Summer Arts Festival is a season of concerts (pop, classical, flamenco), theatre productions, ballets and films – all featuring international as well as Spanish artists. Venues range from theatre and concert halls to the Centro Cultural Conde Duque *(see p64)*.

7 Neighbourhood Festivals

Each neighbourhood *(barrio)* organizes its own celebrations to mark local red-letter days. These range from the blessing of pets in the church of San Antón, Calle Hortaleza (17 January), to Chinese New Year in Lavapiés (end of January/ early February).

8 Festival de Otoño a Primavera
Late Oct–early Jun

For five months each year this major cultural festival promotes the arts with an ambitious programme of dance music, drama and film by international companies. Productions take place in venues across the city.

Production of *Cyrano de Bergerac* for Festival de Otoño a Primavera

9 Virgen de la Almudena
9 Nov

To mark the Feast of the Virgin of Almudena, the image of the patroness of Madrid is carried in procession through the centre of the city, followed by a mass in the cathedral which bears her name *(see p102)*.

10 Christmas Crib Fair
1 Dec–8 Jan

The large Christmas Fair on Plaza Major has more than 100 booths, selling cribs *(belenes)*, Nativity scene figures, trees and decorations.

TOP 10 CELEBRATORY CAKES

Roscón de Reyes

1 Roscón de Reyes
6 Jan
Round buns with almonds and candied fruit, usually containing a small charm.

2 Panecillos de San Antonio
13 Jun
Small rolls marked with a cross are served at the Church of San Antonio.

3 Torrijas
Holy Week
Slices of milk-soaked bread are fried and laced with cinnamon and sugar.

4 Monas de Pascua
Holy Week
Very sweet brioches which are, rather strangely, eaten with hard-boiled eggs.

5 Rosquillas del santo
15 May
Small doughnuts with a variety of flavours and bizarre names – "the fool", "the intelligent one" and "Santa Clara" are just some of them.

6 Suspiros de modistillas
13 Jun
"Needlewomen's sighs" are meringues filled with praline.

7 Huesos de santo
1 Nov
Marzipan sweets sculpted to look like "saints' bones".

8 Buñuelos de viento
1 Nov
Small profiteroles filled with cream, custard or chocolate.

9 Turrón
Christmas
Nougat, hard or soft, and made in various flavours.

10 Polvorones
Christmas
Crumbly biscuits flavoured with cinnamon and almonds.

Madrid
Area by Area

The New Castle of Manzanares el Real at the
foot of the Sierra de Guadarrama mountains

🔟 Around Paseo del Prado

This imposing tree-lined avenue, adorned with fountains and sculptures, is home to no fewer than three world-class art galleries: the Museo Nacional del Prado, the Museo Nacional Centro de Arte Reina Sofía and the Museo Thyssen-Bornemisza. In the 18th century the "prado" was a meadow crossed by a stream, but the rustic surroundings were deceptive, as the area had acquired an unsavoury reputation for muggings and amorous encounters. The solution, devised by Carlos IV, was a stately new boulevard between Plaza de Cibeles and Plaza de Atocha, lined with handsome buildings devoted to the pursuit of scientific investigation. Work began in 1775 on a museum of natural history, which is now the Prado; the botanical gardens and observatory; and a medical school, which is now the Reina Sofía.

Plaza de la Lealtad

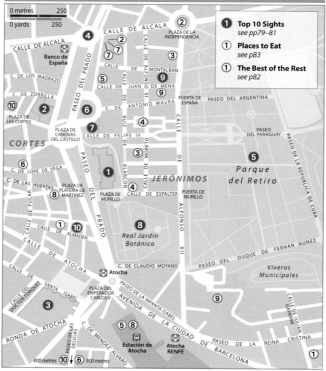

AREA MAP PASEO DEL PRADO

① **Top 10 Sights**
see pp79–81

① **Places to Eat**
see p83

① **The Best of the Rest**
see p82

Palacio de Cibeles on Plaza de Cibeles

1 Museo Nacional del Prado

One of the world's finest art galleries, the Prado includes a spectacular section of Spanish paintings by Francisco Goya within its vast collection (see pp16–21).

2 Museo Thyssen-Bornemisza

What began as a private collection is now a superb public museum of some of the best European art from the past 700 years (see pp28–31).

3 Museo Nacional Centro de Arte Reina Sofía

In contrast to the Prado, this wonderful art gallery is devoted to the very best of 20th- and 21st-century art (see pp32–5).

useo Nacional Centro de Arte Reina Sofía

4 Plaza de Cibeles
MAP F4

One of Madrid's busiest traffic intersections also boasts the city's most famous landmark. The Cibeles Fountain, designed by Ventura Rodríguez, depicts the goddess of nature and abundance riding her chariot, pulled by a pair of prancing lions. (The water-spouting cherubs were added at the end of the 19th century). The most striking architectural monument on the square is the over-the-top Palacio de Cibeles, now the Madrid Town Hall (see p50). Opposite is the Neo-Baroque Palacio de Linares, one of the city's finest 19th-century buildings, and now the Casa de América. On the corner of Calle Recoletos, partly hidden from view by its steeply sloping gardens, is the former Palacio de Buenavista, commissioned in 1777 for the Duchess of Alba, a legendary beauty and one-time lover of artist Francisco Goya. Today it is home to the General Army Barracks.

5 Parque del Retiro

This much-loved city park is a constant source of pleasure to *Madrileños*, especially at weekends and during the hot summer months. There are open spaces to enjoy, as well as wooded areas and formal gardens (see pp36–7).

6 Plaza de la Lealtad

MAP F4 ▪ Madrid Stock Exchange: Plaza de la Lealtad 1; Tours noon on Thu by appointment (email: visitas@grupobme.es to book)

This leafy square honours the fallen heroes of the 1808 uprising against the French *(see p47)*. The ashes of the rebel leaders, immortalized in Goya's famous painting *(see p17)*, were interred in the funerary urns beneath the obelisk when the project was finally completed in 1840. The Neo-Classical building occupying the north side of the square is the Madrid Stock Exchange, designed by Enrique María Repullés in 1884. Visitors may admire the Corinthian-columned façade at any time, but anyone wishing to see the trading floor (with its parquet flooring, painted vaults, stained-glass ceiling and gilded clock) will have to join the guided tour at midday.

CIBELES VERSUS NEPTUNE

These two monuments have earned a place in city folklore and have come to symbolize the rivalry between the city's two main football clubs, Real Madrid and Atlético Madrid. When Real secures a trophy, the team and fans head for the Cibeles statue; when it is the turn of Atlético, Neptune (**right**) is the focus for celebrations. Both fountains have suffered damage over the years so police now impose a cordon, limiting access to the players.

7 Hotel Ritz

MAP F4 ▪ Plaza de la Lealtad 5

The Ritz *(see p142)* first opened its doors in 1910 and the inauguration was attended by King Alfonso XIII, who had backed the project after complaining about the lack of quality accommodation in his capital. French architect Charles Mewes' Neo-Classical building is surprisingly understated from the outside, but the interior is predictably opulent.

Outstanding features include hand-woven carpets from the Royal Tapestry factory and the *belle époque* dining room. Stop for a drink on the terrace.

8 Real Jardín Botánico

MAP F5 ▪ Plaza de Murillo 2 ▪ Open 10am–dusk daily ▪ Closed 1 Jan, 25 Dec ▪ Adm

These delightful gardens were inaugurated in 1781 as a centre for botanical research. Beyond the main entrance is the herbarium – the aromatic, culinary and medicinal plants arranged in separate beds. The central terrace arranges plants by family,

Villanueva Pavilion at the Real Jardín Botánico

species and genealogical history. Look out for the 100-year-old tree known as *"El Pantalones"* due to its resemblance to a pair of inverted trousers – disease has split the trunk in half. Over 1,200 tropical and sub-tropical species are cultivated in the Exhibition Greenhouse, opened in 1993. But the Villanueva Pavilion and the arbours date back to the 18th century.

9 Museo Nacional de Artes Decorativas

MAP G4 ▪ Calle de Montalbán 12
▪ Open Sep–Jun: 9:30am–3pm Tue–Sat, 5–8pm Thu, 10am–3pm Sun; Jul & Aug: 9:30am–3pm Tue–Sat, 10am–3pm Sun ▪ Closed 1 Jan, 6 Jan, 1 May, 9 Nov, 24 Dec, 25 Dec, 31 Dec ▪ Dis. access ▪ Adm (free Thu afternoons)

Housed in a 19th-century mansion overlooking the Retiro is this compelling collection of furniture, silverware, ceramics and glassware from the royal factory of La Granja, as well as jewellery, tapestries, musical instruments, clocks and toys. But the museum is more than a showcase of handicrafts. Arranged chronologically over four floors are reconstructed rooms illustrating Spanish domestic life from the 16th to the early 20th centuries. On the fourth floor is the recreated Valencian kitchen, decorated with over 1,600 hand-painted *azulejo* tiles. The below-stairs life of an 18th-century palace is brought to life to show servants struggling with trays of pies and desserts while the cats steal fish.

10 CaixaForum

MAP F5 ▪ Paseo del Prado 36
▪ Open 10am–8pm daily ▪ Dis. access ▪ Adm to exhibitions (free 15 May, 9 Nov) ▪ Closed 25 Dec, 1 & 6 Jan

It's hard to miss this cultural centre, which is set in a stunningly converted electrical station, crowned by a web of cast iron. Outside, there's an enormous vertical garden, and inside are galleries for excellent temporary exhibitions There are concerts, film screenings, talks and more, and a stylish fourth-floor café that offers a close-up view of the cast-iron shell.

A DAY ON THE PASEO DEL PRADO

▶ MORNING

Begin at **Plaza de Cibeles** *(see p79)* and take a quick peek at the palatial central hall of the **Town Hall** *(see p50)*. Plans to redirect traffic away from the Paseo del Prado have been frustrated, but the central boulevard still provides a pleasant walk, with plenty of shade in summer. Cross the road to **Plaza de la Lealtad** and the garden terrace of the **Hotel Ritz** – a delightful spot for coffee.

Continue past the Neo-Classical façade of the **Museo Nacional del Prado** *(see pp16–21)* and you'll come to Plaza de Murillo and the **Real Jardín Botánico**. Allow at least an hour here to make the most of the verdant tranquillity.

Upon leaving the garden, cross the Paseo del Prado and double back to Plaza Cánovas del Castillo and Ventura Rodríguez's splendid Neptune Fountain. The little side streets here are crammed with plenty of tempting *tapas* bars and restaurants. You could try **La Platería** for a light lunch *(see p83)*.

AFTERNOON

After lunch, take a small detour into Plaza de las Cortes, to admire the impressive portico of the **Congreso de los Diputados** *(see p82)*. Return to Paseo del Prado and on your left is the **Museo Thyssen-Bornemisza** which will occupy the rest of the afternoon *(see pp28–31)*. Take the central boulevard to return to Plaza de Cibeles. Colección Cibeles, the café at the Palacio de Cibeles, is excellent *(see p83)*.

See map on p78

The Best of the Rest

Real Fábrica de Tapices

1 Real Fábrica de Tapices

 ■ MAP H6 ■ Calle Fuenterrabía 2 ■ Open 10am–2pm Mon–Fri ■ Closed 1 Jan, 6 Jan, 1 May, 2 May, Aug, 24–31 Dec ■ Adm

The Royal Tapestry Factory was founded in the 18th century. The artisans still weave using the original wooden looms.

2 Puerta de Alcalá

MAP G4

This imposing Neo-Classical gateway to the city was designed in 1769 by Francisco Sabatini.

3 Iglesia de San Jerónimo el Real

MAP F5 ■ Calle de Moreto 4 ■ Open 9:30/10am–8:30pm Tue–Sun ■ Closed afternoons

The Castilian parliament, the Cortes, met in this historic church in 1510.

4 Salón de Reinos

MAP F4 ■ Méndez Núñez 1 ■ Closed until 2019

The Hall of Kingdoms was part of a 17th-century palace. It has now been acquired by the Museo Nacional del Prado (see pp16–21).

5 Museo Naval

■ MAP F4 ■ Paseo del Prado 5 ■ Open 10am–7pm daily (to 3pm Aug); Jul: 9:30am–2:30pm and 4–6:30pm ■ Closed public hols

Among the highlights here is a 16th-century Flemish galleon and the first map of the New World.

6 Museo del Ferrocarril

 MAP F6 ■ Paseo de las Delicias 61 ■ Open 9:30am–3pm Tue–Fri, 10am–8pm Sat (to 3pm Sun) ■ Closed 1 Jan, 6 Jan, 1 May, 16–31 Aug, 25 Dec ■ Adm

The railway museum has a wonderful collection of old steam locomotives on display and is the departure point for the Tren de la Fresa (see p59).

7 CentroCentro

MAP F4 ■ Plaza de Cibeles 1 ■ www.centrocentro.org ■ Adm

Madrid's former main post office now houses a cultural centre with a spectacular viewing terrace (see p52).

8 Estación de Atocha

MAP F6

The train station combines a sleek modern concourse and a charming 1880s glass-and-iron construction, now housing a lush garden (see p57).

Observatorio Astronómico

9 Observatorio Astronómico

MAP G6 ■ Calle Alfonso XII 3 ■ Open Fri–Sun (by appointment) ■ 91 506 1261, 91 597 9564 ■ Adm

The National Observatory museum includes historic telescopes and other astronomical instruments.

10 Congreso de los Diputados

MAP E4 ■ Carrera de San Jerónimo ■ Open 10:30am–12:30pm Sat ■ Closed Aug, public hols

Admire the portico and Renaissance-style sculptures of the congress building on a guided tour.

Places to Eat

PRICE CATEGORIES
For a three-course meal for one with half
a bottle of wine (or equivalent meal),
taxes and extra charges.

€ under €35	€€ €35–€70	€€€ over €70

1 Matilda Café Cantina
MAP F5 ■ Calle Almadén 15
■ 91 429 0829 ■ €

A cosy place serving home-made
cakes, and lunches made with
market-fresh produce. Later it
becomes an intimate cocktail spot.

2 Restaurante Palacio de Cibeles
MAP F4 ■ Plaza de Cibeles 1,
6th floor ■ 91 523 1454
■ Dis. access ■ €€€

Award-winning chef
Adolfo Muñoz prepares
innovative dishes using
local ingredients. The
terrace offers beautiful
views of Madrid and the
Cibeles fountain.

Restaurante Palacio de Cibeles

3 Horcher
MAP F4 ■ Calle de Alfonso XII 6
■ 91 522 0731 ■ Closed Sat L, Sun,
Easter, Aug, 24 & 31 Dec ■ €€€

One of Madrid's most exclusive
restaurants, Horcher specializes
in Central European cuisine,
particularly game.

Horcher

4 Café del Botánico
MAP F5 ■ Calle Ruiz de Alarcón
27 ■ 91 420 2342 ■ €

Located near the Botanical Gardens,
this elegant restaurant serves a good
selection of drinks and food.

5 Restaurante y Gastrobar Samarkanda
MAP F6 ■ Glorieta de Carlos V, Atocha
Station ■ 91 530 9746 ■ €€

Enjoy Mediterranean cuisine, coffee
and cocktails here.

6 Taberna la Dolores
MAP E4 ■ Plaza de Jesús 4
■ 91 429 2243 ■ €

This classic *taberna* has kept its
original tiled frontage, dating from
1908. The canapés *(pulgas)* are
recommended.

7 Colección Cibeles
MAP F4 ■ Plaza de
Cibeles 1, 2nd floor
■ 91 523 1570 ■ €

This chic, designer café
in the Palacio de Cibeles
offers a great-value set
lunch, and is a handy
spot for a quick lunch
just a stone's throw from
the Prado and Thyssen
museums.

8 La Platería
MAP F5 ■ Moratín 49 ■ 91 429
1722 ■ €

Situated off the Paseo del Prado,
there's a terrace where you can
snack on Castilian dishes such as
jamón Ibérico and goat's cheese
while you watch the world go by.

9 Viridiana
MAP F4 ■ Calle Juan de Mena
14 ■ 91 523 4478 ■ €€€

Master chef Abraham García's bistro
offers a sensational, innovative menu
and a superb wine list *(see p70)*.

10 Bodegas Rosell
MAP F6 ■ Calle General Lacy
14 ■ 91 467 8458 ■ Closed Easter;
Mon L Jun–Oct; Sun D & Mon Nov–
May; Aug ■ €

This classic Madrid tavern serves
great value wines and generous
portions of splendid *tapas*. Booking
is recommended.

See map on p78 ←

🔟 Salamanca and Recoletos

One of Madrid's most affluent neighbourhoods, Salamanca is named after its founder, José de Salamanca y Mayol (1811–83). The Marquis first saw the commercial possibilities of the area in the 1860s and transformed it with grid-patterned streets and elegant mansions. The new neighbourhood was an immediate hit with the upper classes who found the central districts stifling, and their antiquated homes lacking in things such as flushing toilets and hot running water. Salamanca soon acquired a reputation as a bastion of conservatism and its residents were among the most loyal supporters of the Franco regime. Today the streets around Calle de Serrano, Calle de Goya and Calle de Velázquez form Madrid's premier shopping district.

Museo de Escultura al Aire Libre

1 Café Gijón
MAP F3 ▪ Paseo de Recoletos 21 ▪ €€

The haunt of journalists and leading cultural figures, the Gijón was founded in 1888 and is one of the few surviving *tertulia* cafés where, traditionally, men gathered to discuss issues of the day. Former patrons include the poet Federico García Lorca, the American film director Orson Welles and – more improbably – the famous Dutch spy Mata Hari. Order *tapas* and drinks at the bar or book a table for lunch. The windows look on to Paseo de Recoletos where the café has its own terrace.

2 Museo Arqueológico Nacional

The scale of the Archaeological Museum's collections can be daunting, so home in on what interests you most. The star turn on the main floor is the *Lady of Elche*, a stone bust of an Iberian noble-

Lady of Elche

woman from the 4th century BC. There is a niche in the back to hold the ashes of the dead, which is typical of the funerary rites of Iberian culture. Other highlights include a Roman mosaic floor, the Recesvinth crown from the Guarrazar treasure (Toledo, 7th-century) and an ivory cross from the church of San Isidoro in León (1063). The museum was closed for renovation in 2008 and reopened with a redesigned collection in 2014 *(see pp38–9)*.

3 Plaza de Colón
MAP F2

Named after Christopher Columbus, this expansive square commemorates the discovery of the New World. The three monumental slabs near Calle de Serrano symbolize the ships that made the voyage to America in 1492. There is also a conventional sculpture of Columbus, dating from the 19th century. The base shows Queen Isabella I of Castile selling her jewellery to finance the trip.

For a key to restaurant price ranges see p91

AREA MAP OF SALAMANCA AND RECOLETOS

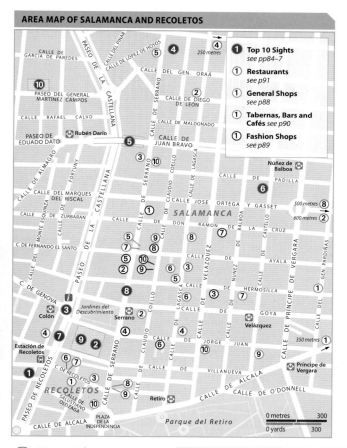

4 **Museo Lázaro Galdiano**
Calle de Serrano 122 ▪ Metro Rubén Darío or Gregorio Marañón ▪ Open 10am–4:30pm Tue–Sat, 10am–3pm Sun ▪ Closed Mon, public hols ▪ Adm (free 2–3pm Sun & 3:30pm–4:30pm Tue–Sat)

José Lázaro Galdiano (1862–1947) was a patron of the arts and a collector whose Italian-style palazzo is now a museum showcasing his fabulous possessions. There are Spanishworks by El Greco, Velázquez and Goya, and European paintings by Constable and Gainsborough. There are spectacular *objets d'art*, too.

Adoration of the Magi, El Greco

5 Museo de Escultura al Aire Libre

MAP G1 ■ Paseo de la Castellana 40

Situated beneath a road bridge, the open-air sculpture museum is easily overlooked. Nevertheless, exhibited in its windswept precincts are works by a number of outstanding modern Spanish sculptors, including Eduardo Chillida, Julio González, Joan Miró and Pablo Serrano.

6 Fundación Juan March

MAP H1 ■ Castelló 77 ■ Open 11am–8pm Mon–Sat, 10am–2pm Sun ■ Closed public hols

One of Spain's most vital cultural institutions was founded in 1955 by the banker Juan March Ordinas, to promote contemporary Spanish art. Madrid shares the permanent collection (especially strong on abstract artists of the 1950s such as Tàpies, Sempere, Saura and Millares) with other branches of the foundation in Cuenca and Palma de Mallorca, but the foundation's main attractions are its outstanding temporary exhibitions (see p65).

7 Paseo de Recoletos

MAP F3

"Paseo" implies a stroll and this lovely avenue, at its best on a sunny morning or just after sunset, was designed precisely for that purpose. The first cafés began to appear in the 19th century when the boulevard was nicknamed "Recoletos beach". Most of the originals had disappeared by the 1980s when the Movida gave the terraces a new lease of life.

Paseo de Recoletos

The Pabellón de Espejo looks the part with its painted tiles and wrought-iron adornments but actually dates from the 1990s. No. 10 was the residence of the Marqués de Salamanca.

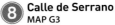

Calle de Serrano

8 Calle de Serrano

MAP G3

Madrid's smartest shopping street runs through the heart of the Salamanca district. Here, top Spanish designer names such as Loewe, Purificación García and Roberto Verino rub shoulders with Armani, Gucci, Yves Saint Laurent and Cartier. Even if you're not especially interested in fashion, there's plenty to amuse you. Madrid's best-known department store, El Corte Inglés, has branches at Nos. 47 and 52, while Agatha Ruíz de la Prada is at No. 27. If you're looking for gifts, visit Adolfo Dominguez's concept store (No. 5), which stocks great gifts, jewellery and accessories. For a bite to eat, try Serrano No. 50 which has a *menú del día*, as well as a selection of *tapas*.

9 Biblioteca Nacional
MAP G3 ■ Paseo de Recoletos 20–22 ■ Open 10am–8pm Mon–Fri, 10am–2pm Sat ■ Free

Founded in 1712 by Felipe V, Spain's National Library is one of the world's largest. It has occupied its current home, an immense Neo-Classical building on Paseo de Recoletos, since the end of the 19th century. Highlights of its collection include 26 rare 17th-century editions of Cervantes' classic, *Don Quixote*, and drawings and etchings by illustrious artists from Goya to Velázquez. The splendid reading rooms are open only to holders of a reader's card, but the exhibition galleries and fascinating museum are open to the public.

10 Museo Sorolla
Paseo del General Martínez Campos 37 ■ Metro Iglesia, Rubén Darío or Gregorio Marañón ■ Open 9:30am–8pm Tue–Sat, 10am–3pm Sun & public hols ■ Closed Mon & some public hols ■ Adm

This museum is devoted to the Valencian artist Joaquín Sorolla y Bastida (1863–1923) who spent the last 13 years of his life here. Some rooms have been left as they were in his lifetime, while others are used to hang his work. Dubbed "the Spanish Impressionist", his subject matter ranges from Spanish folk types to landscapes, but Sorolla is at his most appealing when evoking the sea. Don't leave without seeing the Andalusian-style garden.

The Bathing of the Horse (1909) by Joaquín Sorolla y Bastida

See map on p85 ←

A DAY'S SHOPPING

Isolee • *Cristina Castañer* • *Gino's* • *Calle de Hermosilla*
Teatríz
Serrano Metro Station • *El Jardín de Serrano* • *Estay*
Loewe • *Kenzo* • *Calle de Jorge Juan*
Pedro Garcia
Monasterio Antigüedades
Mallorca • *Capa Sculptures*
Calle de Claudio Coello

▶ **MORNING**

Leave Serrano metro station, heading south and limber up with a spot of window shopping on Salamanca's main fashion drag. Turn left into Calle Columela – try not to pay too much attention to **Pastelería Mallorca's** mouthwatering displays of cakes and pastries *(see p88]* – then left again into Calle Claudio Coello, a delightful street lined with private art galleries, antique shops and boutiques. Don't miss **Capa Sculptures** (No. 19), **Monasterio Antigüedades** (No. 21), **Cristina Castañer** (No. 51) and stylish concept store **Isolée** (No. 55) *(see p89]*. Look left at Calle de Goya for the entrance to the shopping mall, **El Jardín de Serrano** *(see p88]*. Cross Goya, then continue along Calle de Claudio Coello to **Calle de Hermosilla**.

Many Spanish shops take a long lunch break so this is the perfect moment to stop for lunch. Choices abound, but leading contenders include **Teatríz** *(see p91]*, the *tapas* bar at **Estay** *(see p90]* or **Gino's** *(see p91]* for good value Italian food.

AFTERNOON

When you're ready to move on, head south towards the vibrant thoroughfare of Calle Jorge Juan, which boasts a number of designer shops, such as **Pedro Garcia**, **Kenzo** and **Loewe**. Return to **Calle de Serrano**, Madrid's boutique boulevard, where you can either ogle over the designer goods and dream, or blow your budget on a beautiful handbag or a pair of shoes.

General Shops

El Corte Inglés

1 El Corte Inglés
MAP H2 ■ Calle de Goya 76

This branch of Madrid's best-known department store also has a beauty parlour, restaurant and supermarket, as well as the usual departments.

2 El Jardín de Serrano
MAP G2 ■ Calle de Goya 6–8

One of Madrid's most exclusive shopping malls. It has the top names in fashion, accessories and jewellery, as well as a branch of the Mallorca café and delicatessen chain.

3 Galería ABC Serrano
MAP G1 ■ Calle de Serrano 61

Salamanca's other main shopping centre also has a good selection of boutiques (including a branch of the Spanish chain, Mango).

4 Centro de Anticuarios Lagasca
MAP G3 ■ Calle de Lagasca 36

Antiques-lovers can save time traipsing the streets for individual shops by visiting this gallery, which brings together a number of Madrid's most reputable dealers.

5 Santa
MAP G1 ■ Calle de Serrano 56

If you love chocolate, look no further than this tiny outlet on Serrano which also sells gift-wrapped sweets. The speciality here is *leña vieja* (chocolates that are cast to resemble tree trunks).

6 Mercado de la Paz
MAP G2 ■ Calle de Ayala 28

Salamanca's best-known food market is hidden away on this side street and is worth tracking down for its Spanish delicacies, as well as for its surprisingly wide range of international cheese.

7 Vázquez Fruits
MAP G2 ■ Calle de Ayala 11

This small but famous fruit vendor includes, it is said, Queen Sofía among its patrons. The selection of tropical fruits in particular will stir the taste buds.

8 Pastelería Mallorca
MAP G3 ■ Calle de Serrano 6

This reputable delicatessen chain offers a mouth-watering selection of cheese, ham, pastries, filled rolls, cakes and ice cream. Stock up for a picnic, or there's a small bar if you can't tear yourself away.

9 La Studio
MAP H3 ■ Calle de Castelló 8

Rifle through an amazing range of antiques and *objets d'art,* from retro sofas and Art Deco lamps, to original oil paintings and gilded-looking glasses.

El Jardín de Serrano

10 Zara Home
MAP G1 ■ Calle de Serrano 88

Part of the Inditex Group, which also includes the clothing brand of the same name, Zara Home stocks a great range of stylish and affordable household goods.

Fashion Shops

 Alfredo Villalba
MAP G2 ■ Calle de Serrano 68

Spanish celebrities love Alfredo Villalba's luxurious and highly original designs for women, and his dresses, often elaborately beaded, have adorned many a red carpet.

2 Agatha Ruiz de la Prada
MAP G2 ■ Calle de Serrano 27

Men and women's fashions by one of the country's most original designers, noted for her daring use of colour. Her name can also be found on the accessories, stationery and household goods sold here.

3 NAC
MAP G2 ■ Calle de Hermosilla 34

A favourite with Madrid's fashion connoisseurs, NAC selects designs from more than 50 labels to create a chic, urban yet relaxed look.

4 Loewe
MAP G3 ■ Calle de Serrano 26 & 34

Loewe may not sound Spanish, but is in fact one of Spain's longest established names – the first Madrid shop opened in 1846. Renowned for accessories, especially leather.

5 Roberto Verino
MAP G3 ■ Calle de Serrano 33

Men's and women's fashions and accessories by another of Spain's flagship designers. Claims to cater for confident women who know what they want to wear.

6 Angel Schlesser
MAP G2 ■ Callejón Jorge Juan 12

Like Roberto Verino, Spanish designer Angel Schlesser was once labelled "dissident" but has now moved into the mainstream with his distinctive style of clothes and accessories for men and women. Trademarks include low-key colours and attention to detail.

7 Speed and Bacon
MAP G2 ■ Calle Don Ramón de la Cruz 26

This great studio sells shoes, clothes and accessories from up-and-coming Spanish artists and designers such as La Condesa, Yiyi Gutz, Yono Taolo and Leticia Vea.

8 Ursula Mascaró
MAP G3 ■ Claudio Coello 61

Head to this flagship shop where you can discover the flamboyant shoe and handbag designs of Ursula Mascaró.

9 Cristina Castañer
MAP G3 ■ Calle de Claudio Coello 51

Espadrilles are not generally associated with high fashion, but this Spanish designer has turned them into an art form. All colours and styles from casual to evening wear.

10 Isolée
MAP G3 ■ Calle de Claudio Coello 55

One of Madrid's first concept stores, Isolée mixes fashion, design and gourmet food under one roof. It's ultra-hip, from its sleek café to its cool choice of music.

Interior at Loewe

See map on p85

Tabernas, Bars and Cafés

1 Taberna de la Daniela

Calle de General Pardiñas 21 ■ **Metro Goya** ■ **91 575 2329** ■ **€**

This traditional *azulejo*-decorated *taberna* serves a very tempting *tapas* selection. The three-course *cocido* (Madrid stew) is also worth trying.

2 Tasca La Farmacia

MAP G1 ■ **Calle de Diego de León 9** ■ **91 564 8652** ■ **Closed Sun, late Jul–late Aug** ■ **€€**

This former pharmacy has attractive *azulejo* decoration. The house speciality is *bacalao* (cod) prepared in many different ways *(see p68)*.

3 Taberna Embroque

MAP F3 ■ **Calle de Recoletos 17** ■ **91 575 9234** ■ **Closed Sun & Mon** ■ **€**

This charismatic *tapas* bar is decorated with typical *azulejo* and barrels. There are live flamenco performances Thursday to Saturday.

4 El Espejo

MAP F3 ■ **Paseo de Recoletos 31** ■ **91 319 1122** ■ **Closed 24 Dec** ■ **€€**

You can choose between the main restaurant or the elegant terrace and conservatory. The terrace serves only

Taberna de la Daniela

a set menu or *tapas*, and a pianist will serenade you during the summer.

5 Cervecería José Luis

MAP G2 ■ **Calle de Serrano 89** ■ **91 563 0958** ■ **€€**

Attracting a loyal local clientele, the *tapas* here are said to be among the best in the city. The tortilla is heavenly.

6 El Rincón de Goya

MAP G2 ■ **Calle de Lagasca 48** ■ **91 435 7608** ■ **€€**

Decorated with scenes of old Madrid, this popular local serves standards such as the Madrid stew *cocido (see p69)*.

7 Estay

MAP G2 ■ **Calle de Hermosilla 46** ■ **91 578 0470** ■ **Closed Sun** ■ **€**

A bar with a touch of sophistication, Estay offers a selection of imaginatively prepared *tapas* such as French toast with apple compote. The desserts are to die for.

8 O'Caldiño

MAP G2 ■ **Calle Lagasca 74** ■ **91 575 7014** ■ **Closed 1 Jan, 25 Dec** ■ **€€**

This classic *tapas* bar has been serving delicious seafood in an elegant setting since 1973.

9 Pastelería Mallorca

MAP G3 ■ **Calle de Serrano 6, Velázquez 59** ■ **91 577 1859** ■ **€**

This branch of the popular Mallorca chain serves canapés, quiches and other delicious savoury pastries.

10 Ramses

MAP G3 ■ **Plaza de la Independencia 4** ■ **91 435 1666** ■ **€€**

The super-stylish main restaurant at Ramses serves an eclectic mix of international dishes. A terrace offers alfresco dining throughout the year.

The terrace at El Espejo

Restaurants

① La Cesta de Recoletos
MAP F3 ■ Calle de Recoletos 10 ■ 91 140 0696 ■ €€

This restaurant, with two Michelin stars, serves fresh and affordable Spanish fare. Enjoy a quality lunch in less than an hour.

② St James
MAP H1 ■ Calle de Ortega y Gasset 83 ■ 91 402 1583 ■ Closed Sun D ■ €€

Located on a famous street in Madrid, this eatery serves superb Mediterranean cuisine. It is especially renowned for its out-of-this-world rice dishes.

③ La Trainera
MAP G3 ■ Calle de Lagasca 60 ■ 91 576 8035 ■ Closed Sun, Aug ■ €€

Renowned for its fish and seafood. The well thought out Spanish wine selection beautifully complements the fresh daily catches from Galicia. Half portions are perfect for sharing *(see p71)*.

④ Café Oliver
MAP F3 ■ Calle Maria de Molina 50 ■ 91 521 7379 ■ €€

This trendy bar-restaurant with a modern interior serves Mediterranean cuisine and brunch on Sundays. The large windows make it a great spot for people-watching.

⑤ Gino's
MAP G2 ■ Calle de Hermosilla 23 ■ 91 275 8961 ■ €

A popular Italian restaurant chain, Gino's offers a wide selection of pizzas, pasta and meat dishes. The all-inclusive dinner for two on Sundays is especially good value.

⑥ Al-Mounia
MAP G3 ■ Calle de Recoletos 5 ■ 91 435 0828 ■ Closed Sun D, Easter, Aug ■ €€

North African specialities are served at this well-established restaurant. There is belly-dancing on Friday and Saturday nights.

⑦ El Borbollón
MAP F3 ■ Calle de Recoletos 7 ■ 91 431 4134 ■ Closed Sun, public hols ■ €€

Dine on traditional French Basque dishes such as rack of lamb.

⑧ Marisquería El Pescador
MAP H1 ■ Calle de Ortega y Gasset 75 ■ 91 402 1290 ■ Closed Sun ■ €€

This place serves delectable fresh fish and seafood in an intimate setting.

Ramón Freixa Madrid

⑨ Ramón Freixa Madrid
MAP G3 ■ Calle Claudio Coello 67 ■ 91 781 8262 ■ Closed Sun, Mon, Easter, Aug, Christmas ■ €€€

Star chef Ramón Freixa's gastronomic mecca received its second Michelin star in 2010 *(see p71)*.

⑩ Iroco
MAP G3 ■ Calle de Velázquez 18 ■ 91 431 7381 ■ €€

This is Spanish cuisine with a range of influences. Diners pay extra to sit on the terrace.

See map on p85

TOP 10 Downtown Madrid

Central Madrid began to take on its present appearance in the mid-19th century with the modernization of Puerta del Sol. This busy intersection was the first to have electric street lighting, trams and, in 1919, Madrid's first metro station. Meanwhile Calle de Alcalá was becoming the focal point of a new financial district as banks and other businesses set up their headquarters in showy new premises. Building work on the Gran Vía began in 1910 but was only completed in the 1940s with the remodelling of Plaza de España. To make way for this sweeping Parisian-style boulevard, 1,315 m (1,440 yds) long and designed with automobile traffic in mind, more than 300 buildings were demolished and 14 streets disappeared. The new avenue reflected the American architectural tastes of the jazz age, with skyscrapers, cinemas, glitzy cocktail bars, luxury hotels, theatres and restaurants.

Bear climbing an arbutus tree, the symbol of the city

AREA MAP OF DOWNTOWN MADRID

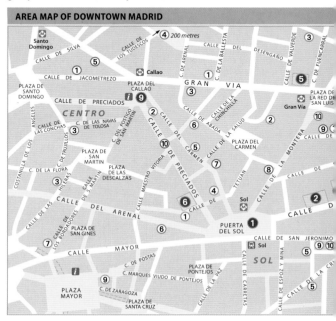

1 Puerta del Sol
MAP N4

Ten streets radiate from this oval-shaped square, which for most *Madrileños* is the real heart of the city. The name actually means "Gateway of the Sun" although the gateway itself was demolished in 1570. Of numerous historic events to take place here, the most dramatic occurred during the 1808 insurrection when snipers fired on one of Napoleon's soldiers, provoking a massacre. Dominating the south side of the square is the 18th-century Casa de Correos, a post office which later became the Ministry of the Interior, and now houses the regional government. A marker in front of the building indicates *"kilómetro cero"*, from which all distances in Spain are calculated. In the centre of the square is a statue of Carlos III and, on the corner of Calle del Carmen, is a bronze statue of a bear climbing an arbutus tree (*madroño* in Spanish) – the symbol of the city.

2 Real Casa de la Aduana
MAP P4 ■ Calle de Alcalá 5, 7, 9 & 11 ■ Closed to public

The royal customs house was a cornerstone of Carlos III's plans to improve the appearance of the city. In 1761, the queen's stables and 16 houses were demolished to make way for Francisco Sabatini's Neo-Classical masterpiece. Enormous amounts of money were lavished on the façade alone, the decorative features of which include ashlar columns and a balcony bearing the royal coat of arms. It is now the head-quarters of the Ministry of Economy and Finance.

Real Casa de la Aduana

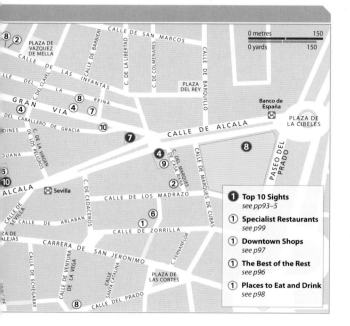

3 Real Academia de Bellas Artes de San Fernando

MAP P3 ■ Calle de Alcalá 13 ■ Open 10am–3pm Tue–Sun & public hols ■ Closed Mon ■ Adm

Founded in the 18th century, the palatial Academy of Fine Arts houses a collection of paintings surpassed only by the Prado and the Thyssen-Bornemisza. Outstanding among the Spanish paintings are the Goyas, including the classic fiesta scene, *Burial of the Sardine*. There are also impressive works by European masters including Bellini, Tintoretto, Van Dyck, Rubens and Titian. Picasso and Dali studied here for a time.

Círculo de Bellas Artes

4 Círculo de Bellas Artes

MAP R3 ■ Calle Alcalá 42 ■ Open 9am–7pm Mon–Thu, 9am–5pm Fri ■ Closed 24, 25 & 31 Dec, 1 Jan ■ Exhibitions closed in Aug ■ Adm

While the golden age of the Fine Arts Club occurred in the 1920s and 1930s, this cultural organization is still thriving today. The Círculo promotes Spanish and world culture, with exhibitions, theatre and ballet productions, art films, workshops and conferences. It even has a magazine and a radio station.

ERNEST HEMINGWAY

The famous American writer Ernest Hemingway arrived in Madrid in March 1937 to find a city under siege. He stayed in the Hotel Florida on Plaza del Callao (since demolished), and recalled dodging shells and sniper bullets on Gran Vía as he made his way to the Telefónica building to file his stories.

---

5 Edificio Telefónica

MAP P2 ■ Calle Fuencarral 3 ■ Open 10am–8pm Tue–Sun ■ Closed Mon, 1 Jan, 6 Jan, 25 Dec, public hols

Now headquarters of Spain's national telephone company, this was Madrid's first high-rise building. Designed by American architect Lewis Weeks and constructed by Ignatio de Cárdenas in 1929, it reflects the values of the Chicago School, then much in vogue. The Telefónica building played an important role in the Civil War when it was used by the Republican army to observe enemy troop movements in the Casa de Campo. Franco's forces found it an ideal range finder for their artillery. The Fundación de Arte y Tecnología Telefónica has an exhibition on the history of communications as well as a splendid art collection, with works by Picasso, Juan Gris and Antoni Tàpies. Another room on the ground floor hosts temporary exhibitions.

6 El Corte Inglés

MAP N3 ■ Calle de Preciados 3

The story of the founder of Spain's premier department store, Ramón Areces Rodríguez, is a classic tale of rags-to-riches. At the age of 15, Areces emigrated to Cuba and worked as a shop assistant before returning to Spain in 1934. The following year he opened a small tailor's in Calle de Preciados and never looked back. It's hard to miss the distinctive white shopping bags with the green logo. There are numerous branches in the capital.

7 Edificio Metrópolis

MAP R3 ■ Corner Gran Vía & Calle de Alcalá

It was La Unión y el Fénix insurance company, the original owners of this Madrid landmark, who commissioned the striking statue on the cupola. Known as *"Ave Fenix"*, it represents the fabled bird that died on a funeral pyre but rose from the flames once every 500 years. When the Metrópolis company moved into the building, it inherited the sculpture, which then lost its significance *(see p50)*.

Banco de España

8 Banco de España
MAP F4 ■ Calle de Alcalá 48

The Bank of Spain was founded in 1856, and 20 years later acquired the exclusive right to issue bank notes in its name. The most impressive part of these headquarters is the corner section, decorated with typical Neo-Baroque ornamentation, a marble clock and the distinctive golden globe. Spain's gold reserves are locked away in the vaults beneath Plaza de Cibeles. Apart from gold, the bank's main treasure is its art collection, with works ranging from Goya to Tàpies. It can be viewed only by written application to the bank.

9 Plaza del Callao
MAP M2

The look of this busy square reflects the sleek modernist architecture of 1930s America. Good examples are the Edificio Cine Callao (No. 3), the Palacio de la Prensa (No. 4), the former headquarters of the Press Association, and the Palacio de la Música (Gran Vía 35), which today houses both the Cine Capitol cinema (see p96) and the Hotel Vincci Capitol.

10 Casino de Madrid
MAP Q3 ■ Calle de Alcalá 15

This exclusive gentlemen's club was founded in 1910. The florid architecture is typical of the period, but the lavish interior is rarely open to the public. Non-members are allowed in the restaurant, La Terraza Del Casino, which has two Michelin stars.

Casino de Madrid

A DAY'S STROLL AROUND DOWNTOWN MADRID

Plaza del Callao • Gran Vía • La Barraca • Edificio Metrópolis • FNAC • Calle de Preciados • Casino de Madrid • Casa de la Aduana • Círculo de Bellas Artes • El Corte Inglés • Puerta del Sol • Calle de Alcalá • Real Academia de Bellas Artes de San Fernando

▶ MORNING

Start the walk outside the Casa de Correos in **Puerta del Sol** (see p93), a popular meeting point for madrileños. Cross the square in the direction of the bus stops, then turn on to Calle de Alcalá. This busy street is lined with fine examples of 18th- and 19th-century architecture. Two examples on your left are the **Real Casa de la Aduana** and the **Real Academia de Bellas Artes de San Fernando**. Take time to visit this often overlooked gallery, with its small, but quality, collection of paintings. Next door is the showy façade of the **Casino de Madrid**.

Cross Calle de Alcalá when you reach the junction with Gran Vía, then head for coffee in the **Círculo de Bellas Artes**. As you make your way back to Gran Vía look up to admire the **Edificio Metrópolis** building, then take a stroll along Madrid's bustling main avenue.

When you're ready for lunch, escape the crowds by turning into Calle de Hortaleza, then Calle de la Reina. At No. 29 is **La Barraca**, famous for its paellas.

AFTERNOON

Head back to Gran Vía and continue to **Plaza del Callao**. Turn left into Calle de Preciados, a pedestrianized street that is dominated by its two large department stores, **FNAC** (see p97) and **El Corte Inglés**.

After a leisurely browse around the shops, return to Puerta del Sol as it begins to liven up for the evening.

See map on pp92–3

The Best of the Rest

 Berlin Café
MAP M2 ■ Calle Jacometrezo 4
■ Closed Mon

This is one of Madrid's best venues for live music, with an eclectic programme which features everything from salsa and reggae to jazz and flamenco. Concerts are followed by DJ sessions.

2 Cine Estudio Círculo de Bellas Artes
MAP E4 ■ Calle Marques de la Casa Riera 4

The cinema of the fine arts centre *(see p94)* shows classic movies by 20th-century directors such as Eisenstein, Fassbinder, Francis Ford Coppola and John Huston.

3 Palacio de la Música
MAP N2 ■ Gran Via 35

The Palacio de la Música occupies a landmark cinema from 1926, which sadly closed after almost 80 years. Its striking Art Deco façade remains unchanged, although the building's future purpose has yet to be decided. More than 80,000 people have signed a petition calling for it to be restored and reopened, as its name suggests, as the Palace of Music.

4 Centro del Ejército y la Armada (Casino Militar)
MAP Q3 ■ Gran Via 13

This elegant building, inaugurated in 1916, has Modernista twirls and is home to a military cultural association. Its graceful salons are used for concerts, dances and talks.

5 Cine Capitol
MAP M2 ■ Gran Vía 41

Located in the Art Deco Carrión building, this cinema's greatest moment occurred early in the Civil War when Eisenstein's stirring movie *Kronstadt* was shown to an audience that included the President of the Republic and leading military figures. Films are screened in Spanish. There are three screens that include digital 3D technology.

 Teatro de la Zarzuela
MAP R4 ■ Calle de Jovellanos 4

Purpose-built to showcase Spain's unique light opera form, *Zarzuela*, this theatre also hosts international opera, music recitals and other events *(see p64)*.

7 Iglesia de Nuestra Señora del Carmen
MAP N3 ■ Calle Carmen 10

This early 17th-century church contains a much-venerated statue of the Virgin, which is paraded around the city on the saint's feast day (16 July), and a rather gory, but equally revered, Baroque statue of the Recumbent Christ.

8 Santería Milagrosa
MAP P3 ■ Calle San Alberto 1

A fascinating emporium near Sol, dealing in all things spiritual – everything from amulets and birth charts to tarot cards, icons and books on white magic.

9 El Sol
MAP P3 ■ Calle de los Jardines 3 ■ Closed Sun & Mon

El Sol is the venue for concerts by Spanish and international bands that date from the Movida period of cultural change in the late 1970s. Reasonable bar and entry prices.

10 Calle Preciados
MAP N3–N4

One of the most popular shopping streets in central Madrid, this pedestrianized artery is home to chains such as El Corte Inglés, FNAC and Zara.

Shoppers on Calle Preciados

Downtown Shops

1 Zara
MAP N2 ■ Gran Vía 34

This Spanish fashion phenomenon is now also a household name throughout Europe and the United States. Stylish clothes for all the family at very reasonable prices.

Branch of Zara on Gran Vía

2 FNAC
MAP N3 ■ Calle de Preciados 28

This useful store, just a few minutes' walk from Puerta del Sol, sells everything from CDs and sound systems to cameras, DVDs, books and mobile phones. There are helpful floor staff, some of whom speak a little English.

Shopfront of FNAC

3 Horno San Onofre
MAP P2 ■ Calle de S Onofre 3

The decor of this traditional Madrid bakery borders on the palatial. The products are just as good – every conceivable type of bread, as well as seasonal specialities such as *roscón de Reyes* and *turrón*.

4 Ariel Real Madrid
MAP N4 ■ Calle Carmen 3

A place of pilgrimage for Real Madrid's army of fans, Los Blancos (The Whites), this shop sells football strips, footballs and plenty of souvenirs.

5 02
MAP N3 ■ Calle del Carmen 14

Raid this store near Puerta del Sol for glitzy costume jewellery and equally showy accessories. Head for the first floor for imaginative gift ideas.

6 Casa de Diego
MAP R4 ■ Calle Mesoneros Romanos 4

This charmingly old-fashioned shop has been in operation for more than 150 years. The beautiful wood-panelled interior is packed with umbrellas and elegant walking canes, along with traditional fans, shawls and pretty hair combs.

7 Loewe
MAP E4 ■ Gran Vía 8

If you are a fan of the Spanish brand Loewe, then head to Gran Vía 8. This is the original store that opened in 1939. Check out its guestbook whose signatories include Grace Kelly.

8 El Elefante Blanco
MAP R2 ■ Calle de las Infantas 5

Shades of the Big Top in this small shop, founded by a former circus performer. It sells all the paraphernalia – including stilts, jugglers' clubs and diabolos. Great for kids.

9 Antigua Relojería
MAP N4 ■ Calle La Sal 2

Established in 1880, this shop specializes in watches. Its interior still has original 1930s wooden cabinets and drawers, and there's a clock featuring a jolly watch-maker outside.

10 Grassy
MAP R3 ■ Gran Vía 1

This famous jeweller occupies one of the signature buildings of the Gran Vía dating from 1916. The gleaming window displays of rings, watches and other items (all original designs) are equally distinguished.

See map on pp92–3

Places to Eat and Drink

1 Casa Labra
MAP N4 ■ Calle de
Tetuán 12 ■ 91 531 0081 ■ €

A Madrid institution, it was
where Pablo Iglesias Posse
founded the Spanish
Workers' Party in 1879. Of the
tapas on offer, try the house
speciality, *soldaditos de Pavía*
(fried cod) *(see p69)*.

Tapas at
Fatigas del
Querer

2 Artemisa
MAP P3 ■ Calle de las Tres
Cruces 4 ■ 91 521 8721 ■ €

This well-known vegetarian
restaurant features a nettle purée
among other imaginative dishes. It
has organic wines and herbal teas.

3 El Escarpín
MAP M3 ■ Calle de las Hileras
17 ■ 91 559 9957 ■ €

This lively Asturian tavern serves
regional specialities such as *fabada*
(bean soup) and *chorizo a la sidra*
(sausages in cider).

4 Museo Chicote
MAP Q3 ■ Gran Vía 12 ■ 91 532
6737 ■ Closed Mon, Aug ■ €€

Ernest Hemingway put this cocktail
bar on the map in the 1930s; other
famous visitors included Frank
Sinatra and Orson Welles *(see p66)*.

Cocktails and tapas at Museo Chicote

5 Fatigas del Querer
MAP P4 ■ Calle de la
Cruz 17 ■ 91 523 2131
■ No credit cards ■ €

This Andalusian tavern
was built in 1920. There is
an excellent range of *tapas*
on offer, including hearty
raciones, Iberian ham,
seafood and fresh, fried fish.
The atmosphere is always lively,
especially at night *(see p51)*.

6 La Terraza del Casino
MAP Q3 ■ Calle Alcalá 15
■ 91 532 1275 ■ Closed Sun, Mon &
public hols ■ €€€

This two-Michelin-starred restaurant
in Madrid's historic casino features a
terrace with panoramic views, and
some of the finest cuisine in Spain.

7 Yerbabuena
MAP M4 ■ C/Bordadores 3
■ 91 599 4805 ■ Closed Sun D ■ €

This bright, cheery café offers
vegetarian, vegan and coeliac-
suitable fare – all still quite rare
in Madrid.

8 Bar Cock
MAP R3 ■ Calle de la Reina 16
■ 91 532 2826 ■ €€

This tastefully decorated late-night
bar is a good place in which to round
off the evening.

9 Museo del Jamon
MAP P4 ■ Carrera de San
Jerónimo 6 ■ 91 521 0346 ■ €

Snack on delicious cold cuts,
cheeses, cakes and sandwiches
at this restaurant and delicatessen.

10 Priorità Art Coffee Shop
MAP R3 ■ Calle de la Montera
■ 91 531 4037 ■ €

A friendly, arty, simple café,
where you can enjoy inexpensive
drinks and snacks and admire
the changing art exhibitions on
the walls.

Specialist Restaurants

Bright dining room at Al Natural

1 Al Natural

MAP R4 ▪ Calle de Zorilla 11 ▪ 91 369 4709 ▪ Closed Sun D ▪ €

At this unpretentious eatery that serves vegetarian dishes, the house speciality is *tarta de setas y espinacas* (mushroom and spinach and tart).

2 Zara
MAP R2 ▪ Calle de las Infantas 5 ▪ 91 532 2074 ▪ Closed Sat, Sun, public hols, Aug, ▪ €

Just off the Gran Vía, Zara has been a rallying point for Cuban exiles since the 1960s. It serves Caribbean standards such as *ropa vieja* (stewed meat in a rich tomato sauce) and great daiquiris.

3 Cornucopia
MAP M4 ▪ Calle Navas de Tolosa 9 ▪ 91 521 3896 ▪ €

This American-run, art-filled restaurant gives a transatlantic treatment to traditional Spanish fare, with special offer menus and great desserts.

4 El Pez Gordo

MAP N1 ▪ Calle de Pez 6 ▪ 91 522 3208 ▪ €

Formerly a *tasca*, this friendly eatery is excellent for enjoying beer or wine along with a range of delicious tapas. Order the roasted aubergines and you won't be disappointed.

5 La Pulpería de Victoria
MAP P4 ▪ Calle Victoria 2 ▪ 91 080 4929 ▪ €

Specialities at this Galician restaurant include *pulpo a feira* (octopus), cooked in front of the customer, and *empanada* (meat-filled pastry).

6 Ferpal
MAP R4 ▪ Calle de Arenal 7 ▪ 91 532 3899 ▪ Closed Sun ▪ €

This charcuterie near Sol has the usual range of *jamón Ibérico*, pâtés and cheeses, as well as sandwiches. Eat at the bar or take away.

7 La Venganza de Malinche
MAPP3 ▪ Calle Jardines 5 ▪ 91 523 4164 ▪ Closed Sun D ▪ €

Colourful decor, friendly staff and a great range of spicy tacos, burritos and other regional specialities. The set lunch is a bargain.

8 Villa Paramesa Prado
MAP R5 ▪ Calle del Prado 15 ▪ 91 429 0351 ▪ Closed Sun D, Mon ▪ €€

A local favourite, this bar features wooden decor and elaborate dishes. The serving staff is very friendly.

9 La Pecera
MAP R3 ▪ Calle Alcalá 42 ▪ 91 360 5400 ▪ €

For a small entrance fee you can enjoy tea in the café of the Círculo de Bellas Artes *(see p50)*.

10 Lhardy
MAP P4 ▪ Carrera de San Jerónimo 8 ▪ 91 522 2207 ▪ Closed Sun & public hols D ▪ €€€

At this Madrid institution some customers never get further than the *tapas* counter downstairs *(see p70)*.

See map on pp92–3

🔟 Royal Madrid

To wander around this part of Madrid is to be reminded constantly of its regal associations. The magnificent Monasterio de las Descalzas Reales and the Monasterio de la Encarnación are both royal foundations, dating from the Habsburg era (1516–1700), while work on the breathtaking Palacio Real, inspired by the Louvre in Paris, began during the first reign of Felipe V (1700–25). Joseph Bonaparte was King of Spain for only five years (1808–13), but he laid out the plans for the handsome Plaza de Oriente next to the palace. Further afield, the Ermita de San Antonio de la Florida was commissioned by Carlos IV.

Madonna at Monasterio de las Descalzas Reales

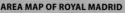

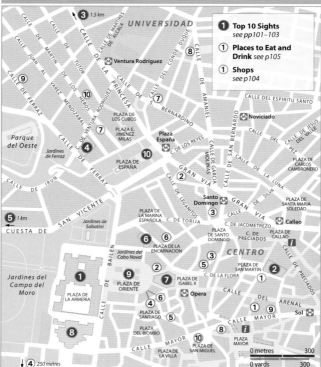

AREA MAP OF ROYAL MADRID

1 **Top 10 Sights**
see pp101–103

1 **Places to Eat and Drink** see p105

1 **Shops**
see p104

Spectacular façade of the Palacio Real

1 Palacio Real

Spain's magnificent palace dominates the area *(see pp12–15)*.

2 Monasterio de las Descalzas Reales

This 16th-century convent is a treasure trove of art *(see pp24–5)*.

3 Museo de América

Avenida Reyes Catótilcos 6 ▪ 91 54 92641 ▪ Open 9:30am–3pm Tue–Sat (to 7pm Thu), 10am–3pm Sun & public hols ▪ Closed 1 & 6 Jan, 1 May, 24, 25 & 31 Dec and one local holiday ▪ www.mecd.gob.es/museodeamerica ▪ Dis. access ▪ Adm

Spain's links with the American continent have a long history, and this wonderful museum displays artifacts from all eras, including textiles, ceramics and art *(see p48)*.

Museo de América

4 Museo Cerralbo

MAP J1 ▪ Calle de Ventura Rodríguez 17 ▪ Open 9:30am–3pm Tue–Sat, 5–8pm Thu, 10am–3pm Sun & public hols ▪ Closed Mon, 1 & 6 Jan, 1 May, 24, 25 & 31 Dec and one local holiday ▪ Dis. access ▪ Adm (free 2–3pm Sat, 5–8pm Thu, Sun)

Don Enrique de Aguilera y Gamboa, Marqués de Cerralbo (1845–1922) was a poet, a politician and a compulsive collector, searching the world for artistic treasures that would adorn his palatial home. He bequeathed his collection to the state so that it could be enjoyed by others. Highlights include a *majolica* Nativity by Renaissance artist Andrea della Robbia (in the Porcelain Room) and El Greco's *Ecstasy of St Francis* (in the Sacristy), but the undoubted *pièce de résistance* is Juderías Caballero's *History of Dance* in the dome of the ballroom *(see p48)*.

5 Ermita de San Antonio de la Florida

Glorieta de San Antonio de la Florida 5 ▪ Open 9:30am–8pm Tue–Sun ▪ Closed Mon, public hols ▪ Dis. access

This hermitage, dedicated to St Anthony of Padua, was completed in 1798. Goya began work on his sublime frescoes in June, and by December they were finished. On St Anthony's Day (13 June) unmarried girls would come to the hermitage to ask the saint to find them a husband.

6 Monasterio de la Encarnación

MAP K3 ▪ Plaza de la Encarnación 1 ▪ Open 10am–2pm, 4–6:30pm Tue–Sat, 10am–3pm Sun & public hols ▪ Closed 1 & 6 Jan, 1–4 Apr, 1 May, 24, 25 & 31 Dec ▪ Adm

The convent was founded in 1611 by Margarita of Austria, wife of Felipe III, for daughters of the nobility. It was also the church of the Alcázar – a picture gallery linked the two buildings. Unfortunately, when the castle was destroyed by fire in 1734 the flames spread to the convent and many of its treasures were lost. A great deal remains however: 17th-century paintings by Ribera and Luca Giordano; impressive sculptures, such as *Recumbent Christ* by Gregorio Fernández; embroidered vestments and gold and silverware. The guided tour takes in the cloister with its decoration of Talavera *azulejos*; the reliquary, where visitors are shown the phial containing the congealed blood of St Pantaleon; the carved stalls in the choir; and the church, designed by Ventura Rodríguez.

7 Teatro Real

MAP K3 ▪ Plaza Isabel II ▪ Open for tours 10:30am–1pm daily ▪ Closed 1 Jan, Aug, 25 Dec ▪ Dis. access ▪ Adm (under 7s free)

The city's state-of-the-art opera house re-opened in 1998 after a lengthy and expensive restoration. There were so many delays in constructing the original theatre that the architect, Antonio López

Teatro Real

THE VIRGIN OF ALMUDENA

A niche in the wall next to the cathedral contains a statue of the Virgin (below). According to legend, the original was hidden from the Moors in the 8th century. More than 300 years later, it was rediscovered by Alfonso VI when part of the city wall fell away. On 9 November the statue is carried from the cathedral in solemn procession (see p75).

Aguado, was long dead before the official opening in 1850 on Queen Isabella II's birthday. Giuseppe Verdi wrote his opera *The Force of Destiny* for the Teatro Real in 1863 – he stayed at No.6 Plaza de Oriente. The dimensions of the restored opera house are impressive: the architects calculate that the back-stage area is large enough to contain the huge Telefónica building on Gran Vía *(see p64)*.

8 Catedral de la Almudena

MAP J4 ▪ Calle de Bailén 10 ▪ Open 9am–8:30pm daily ▪ Dis. access ▪ Museum & dome: open 10am–2:30pm Mon–Sat ▪ Adm

There were plans to build a cathedral on the superb hilltop site in the 18th century, but it was not until 1879 that the Marqués de Cubas got the go-ahead for his ambitious design; even then, only the Romanesque-style crypt was built. The cathedral was finally completed In the 1980s by architect Fernando Chueca Goitia and opened by Pope John Paul II in 1993. The Gothic interior comes as a surprise, as the exterior is Neo-

Classical to harmonize with the Palacio Real. The magnificent bronze doors were installed in October 2000.

9 Plaza de Oriente
MAP K3

The focal point of this beautiful square is the bronze equestrian statue of Felipe IV, moved here from the Buen Retiro palace in 1842. The sculptor Pietro Tacca took advice from Galileo Galilei on the modelling of the rearing horse – the figure of the king was based on sketches by Velázquez. The statues of Spanish rulers were intended for the balustrade of the Palacio Real but they did not meet with royal approval.

10 Plaza de España
MAP K1

A set piece from the Franco era, the huge square at the bottom of the Gran Vía is dominated by Madrid's first skyscrapers, erected in the 1950s. In the centre, a monument to Cervantes features bronze statues of Don Quixote and his faithful companion Sancho Panza. Just visible off the northwest corner of the square is the splendid Templo de Debod, erected in the 2nd century BC near Aswan in Egypt and rebuilt here in 1972. Behind it, leafy Parque del Oeste (see pp56–7) is an ideal spot for a picnic.

Plaza de España

A DAY IN ROYAL MADRID

▶ MORNING

Catch the first guided tour of the morning (10:30am) at the **Monasterio de las Descalzas Reales** (see pp24–5). On leaving, cross Plaza San Martín to Calle de Hilera, then turn right onto Calle del Arenal. Follow this busy street to Plaza de Isabel II, the best place to admire Madrid's opera house, the **Teatro Real**. Follow Calle Felipe V alongside the theatre until you come to **Plaza de Oriente** and the **Palacio Real** (see pp12–15. The palace is closed at least once a week for official functions but, if it is open, it is worth allocating an hour to looking around.

There are plenty of places to eat in the vicinity of **Plaza de Oriente**, for example the café of the same name (see p105). A plaque on the wall nearby reminds visitors that this was once the treasury house where the artist Velázquez had his studio.

AFTERNOON

After lunch, walk over to the **Templo de Debod**. Beautifully reflected in a shallow pool, this temple was a gift to Madrid from the Egyptian government in the 1970s. Continue walking beyond the temple into the quiet, shady paths of the **Parque del Oeste**, where you'll find the cable car (teleférico) to the Casa de Campo. From the cable car station, stroll about 30 minutes through the park to reach the lake (follow signs for lago), where you can hire a rowing boat or enjoy a drink at one of the cafés.

See map on p100 ←

Shops

Records for sale at La Metralleta

1 La Metralleta
MAP M3 ■ Plaza de las Descalzas s/n

This large store specializes in second-hand records. Every taste and period is catered for and the staff are helpful and knowledgeable.

2 Cántaro
MAP L1 ■ Calle Flor Baja 8

A treasure trove for admirers of pottery and an excellent place to shop for gifts. Products from all over Spain at very reasonable prices.

3 Antigua Casa Talavera

MAP L2 ■ Calle de Isabel La Católica 2

If you've been bowled over by the 18th-century Talavera ceramics in the Palacio Real, you'll find that the modern descendants of these craftsmen have not lost their touch. This outlet offers a wide range of hand-painted jugs, plates, mugs and more (see p72).

4 Manuel González Contreras

MAP M4 ■ Calle Segovia 57

This historic workshop is where true guitar enthusiasts come to buy a handcrafted instrument (see p72).

5 El Flamenco Vive
MAP L4 ■ Calle Conde de Lemos 7

This family business specializes in all things flamenco, from beautiful dresses, dance shoes and shawls to guitars and castanets, as well as CDs, DVDs, sheet music and books (see pp72–3).

6 El Obrador del Café de Oriente
MAP K4 ■ Plaza de Oriente 2

If you're planning a picnic in the Sabatini Gardens or further afield, the delicatessen of the Café de Oriente has everything you need, from fresh bread and filled rolls to cheeses, cooked meats and cakes.

7 Ocho y Medio
MAP J1 ■ Calle de Martín de los Heros 11

Located in the centre of Madrid's main cinema district, this shop is a treasure house for film buffs, with books, posters, postcards and more.

8 Kukuxumusu
MAP M4 ■ Calle Mayor 47

This design company started as three friends selling T-shirts on the streets of Pamplona during the 1989 Sanfermines fiesta. The bright graphics proved hugely popular, and Kukuxumusu now sells its products throughout Europe.

9 El Riojano
MAP M4 ■ Calle Mayor 10

Founded in 1855, this pretty, old-style *pastelería* caters for none other than the Spanish royal family. Shop here for seasonal Madrid specialities such as *tocino de cielo*, a silky-smooth *flan*, or *crème caramel*, whose name means "bacon of heaven".

10 Toni Martin Discos
MAP J1 ■ Calle de Martín de los Heros 18

Fans of country music, jazz and rock and roll take note. This excellent outlet has a great selection of CDs and vinyl – new and second-hand.

Places to Eat and Drink

PRICE CATEGORIES

For a three-course meal for one with half a bottle of wine (or equivalent meal), taxes and extra charges.

€ under €35   €€ €35–€70   €€€ over €70

1 Chocolatería San Ginés
MAP M4 ▪ Pasadizo de S Ginés 5 ▪ 91 365 6546 ▪ Always open ▪ €

Head here after a night out for a traditional breakfast of *chocolate con churros*.

2 Taberna del Alabardero
MAP K3 ▪ Calle de Felipe V 6 ▪ 91 547 2577 ▪ Open 1–4pm, 8:30–11:30pm daily ▪ €€

Snack on *jamón Ibérico* or *croquetas* in the *tapas* bar, or eat Basque food in the adjoining restaurant.

3 Santo Restaurant & Deli
MAP L3 ▪ C/Caños del Peral 9 ▪ 91 542 0050 ▪ Closed Mon ▪ €

This friendly eatery serves Brazilian and Mediterranean cuisine. Sunday brunch is fabulous and very popular.

Al Santo Restaurant & Deli

4 Café de Oriente
MAP K3 ▪ Plaza de Oriente 2 ▪ 91 541 3974 ▪ €€

An elegant café with velvet seats, a stucco ceiling and summer terrace.

5 Entre Suspiro y Suspiro
MAP L3 ▪ Calle de Caños del Peral 3 ▪ 91 542 0644 ▪ Closed Sun, 22 Dec, 25 Dec ▪ €€

Delicious Mexican dishes include "devil salad" with prawns, mango, coriander and chicken in chocolate sauce *(mole)*.

Exterior of La Bola Taberna

6 La Bola Taberna
MAP L2 ▪ Calle de la Bola 5 ▪ 91 547 6930 ▪ Closed Sun D, 24 Dec ▪ No credit cards ▪ €

Cocido (various meats cooked in a rich broth) is the highlight at this 19th-century restaurant.

7 El Jardín Secreto
MAP R3 ▪ Calle Conde Duque 2 ▪ 91 541 8023 ▪ €

A well-kept secret in downtown Madrid, with a terrace café offering light meals amid an oasis of greenery.

8 El Cangrejero
MAP C2 ▪ Calle de Amaniel 25 ▪ 91 548 3935 ▪ Closed Sun D ▪ €

This bar has a good choice of sea-food *tapas*. Mahou beer originally came from the factory next door.

9 Entrevinos
MAP J1 ▪ Calle de Ferraz 36 ▪ 91 548 3114 ▪ Closed 1 Jan, 6 Jan, Aug, 24 Dec, 25 Dec, 31 Dec ▪ €

Speciality snacks include *habas* (salted broad beans) with *jamón Ibérico*. The wine list is excellent.

10 Mercado de San Miguel
MAP L5 ▪ Plaza de San Miguel ▪ 91 542 4936 ▪ Open 10am–midnight Sun–Wed, 10am–2pm Thu–Sat (to 7pm on 24 & 31 Dec), noon–midnight on 25 Dec & 1 Jan ▪ €

This renovated early 20th-century market is where the best shops have stalls, selling cheese, ham, sushi, foie gras and pastries.

See map on p100

🔟 Old Madrid

In the 17th century, the focus of the rapidly growing city shifted from the medieval centre around Plaza de la Paja to Plaza Mayor. Part meeting place, part market, this magnificent square was, above all, a place of spectacle and popular entertainment. Over time the houses deteriorated into slums and tenements, while the parishes to the south of Plaza Mayor were home to Madrid's labouring classes. Mingling with the slaughterhouse workers and tanners of the Rastro were market traders, builders, innkeepers, horse-dealers and members of the criminal underclass.

Plaza de la Paja bronze

AREA MAP OF OLD MADRID

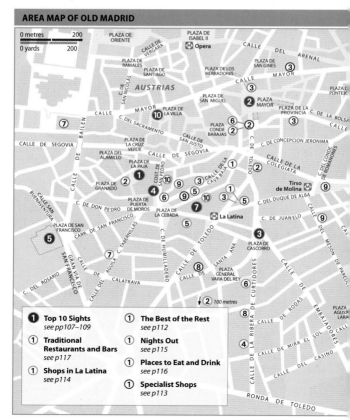

	Top 10 Sights *see pp107–109*	①	The Best of the Rest *see p112*
①	Traditional Restaurants and Bars *see p117*	①	Nights Out *see p115*
①	Shops in La Latina *see p114*	①	Places to Eat and Drink *see p116*
		①	Specialist Shops *see p113*

1 Plaza de la Paja
MAP K6

This was the central square and marketplace of medieval Madrid, later eclipsed by the Plaza Mayor. Today, it is one of the prettiest corners of the city, flanked by hand-some palaces and cafés that spill into the square in summer. At its northern end is the magnificent Capilla del Obispo (the Bishop's Chapel), erected in 1535 as a burial place for San Isidro (whose remains were eventually buried in the Cathedral de San Isidro in the 18th Century). The chapel contains a splendid Renaissance altarpiece as well as the elaborate tombs of *Madrileño* aristocrats.

Plaza Mayor

2 Plaza Mayor

The heart of Old Madrid is this vast square, surrounded by arcaded buildings, now home to a good choice of tourist shops, over-priced restaurants and numerous street entertainers (see pp22–3).

3 El Rastro

You can easily lose a day wandering around the quirky stalls of the city's flea market (see pp26–7) or watching the world go by from the many bars and cafés of the surrounding La Latina quarter.

4 Museo de los Orígenes (Casa de San Isidro)

MAP K6 ■ Plaza de S Andrés 2 ■ Open 9:30am–8pm Tue–Sun & public hols; Aug: 9:30am– 2:30pm Tue–Fri (to 8pm Sat, Sun & public hols) ■ Closed Mon, 1 & 6 Jan, 1 May, and 24, 25 & 31 Dec

The museum is housed in an attractive 16th-century palace, which once belonged to the Count of Paredes. The original Renaissance courtyard is best viewed from the first floor, where archaeological finds from the Madrid region are exhibited, including a Roman mosaic floor from the 4th century. Downstairs, visitors can see wooden models of the city and its royal palaces as they were in the 17th century. A short film is shown bringing to life Francisco Rizi's painting of the 1680 *auto-de-fé* (see p23) and the San Isidro chapel, which was built in the early 17th century near the saint's alleged home.

5 Real Basílica de San Francisco el Grande

MAP B5 ▪ Calle San Buenaventura
▪ **Open** 10:30am–12:30pm, 4–6pm
Tue–Sat; Jul–Sep: 10:30am–12:30pm,
5–7pm Tue–Fri ▪ Adm

Legend has it that this magnificent basilica occupies the site of a monastery founded by St Francis of Assisi in the 13th century. Work on the present building was completed in 1784 under the supervision of Francisco Sabatini. The focal point of the unusual circular design is the stupendous dome, 58 m (190 ft) high and 33 m (110 ft) in diameter. After 30 years of restoration, the 19th-century ceiling frescoes, painted by leading artists, are now revealed in their original glory. Take the guided tour to be shown other treasures, including the Gothic choir paintings by Goya and Zurbarán.

6 Lavapiés
MAP D6

This colourful working-class neighbourhood has a cosmopolitan feel, thanks to its ethnic mix of Moroccans, Indians, Turks and Chinese. The narrow streets sloping towards the river from Plaza Tirso de Molina are full of shops selling everything from cheap clothes and leather handbags to tea and spices. Check out traditional bars such as Taberna Antonio Sánchez *(see p68)*. Performances of the light opera *zarzuela* are given outdoors in La Corrala on Calle Mesón de Paredes 64 in the summer.

7 La Latina
MAP L6

Historic La Latina really comes alive on Sundays when the trendy bars of Cava Baja, Calle de Don Pedro and Plaza de los Carros are frequented by pop singers, actors and TV stars. Plaza de la Paja – the main square of medieval Madrid – takes its name from the straw which was sold here by villagers from the across the River Manzanares. Nowadays it's much quieter and a good place to rest one's legs. The two churches of San Andrés and San

Pedro el Viejo have been restored. Their history, and that of the area as a whole, is explained in the Museo de los Orígenes *(see p107)*.

Bar in Cava Baja, La Latina

8 Casa-Museo de Lope de Vega

MAP R5 ▪ Calle de Cervantes 11
▪ **Open** for tours in English 10am–6pm
Tue–Sun (call 91 429 9216 to book in
advance) ▪ Closed public hols

The greatest dramatist of Spain's Golden Age lived in this house from 1610 until his death in 1635. Lope de Vega started writing at the age of 12, leaving a total of 1,500 plays plus poetry, novels and devotional works. He became a priest after the death of his second wife in 1614, but that didn't stop his philandering, which led to more than one run-in with the law. To tour the restored house with its heavy wooden shutters, creaking staircases and beamed ceilings is to step back in time. Evocative details include a cloak and sword left by one of his friends in the guest bedroom.

SAN ISIDRO

When the future patron saint of Madrid died around 1170 he was buried in a pauper's grave. But, in the 17th century, an unseemly rivalry developed between the clergy of San Andrés and the Capilla de San Isidro over the custody of his mortal remains. The wrangle dragged on until the 18th century, when the body of the saint was interred in the new Catedral de San Isidro, where it has remained ever since.

9 Plaza de Santa Ana
MAP P5

The streets around this well-known square boast the greatest concentration of *tapas* bars in the city and are often still buzzing at 4am. The stylish hotel ME Madrid dominates the square, and there is an amazing view of the Teatro Español opposite from its penthouse bar.

10 Casa de la Villa
MAP K5 ▪ Plaza de la Villa 5
▪ Open for guided tour 5pm Mon

Madrid's city hall was inaugurated in 1692, and remained the seat of the city council until 2008. Its austere façade, steepled towers and ornamental portals are typical of the architectural style favoured by the Habsburgs. Juan de Villanueva added the balcony overlooking Calle Mayor so that Queen María Luisa could watch the annual Corpus Christi procession. Highlights of the tour include a staircase hung with tapestries designed by Rubens, the painted ceiling in the reception hall, the 16th-century silver monstrance carried in the Corpus Christi processions and the debating chamber with frescoes by Antonio Palomino. The Casa de la Villa forms part of an ensemble of historic buildings overlooking the Plaza de la Villa: Casa y Torre de los Lujanes is Madrid's oldest surviving civil building (15th century), and Casa de Cisneros was built for an aristocratic family.

Casa de la Villa

A MORNING WALK AROUND OLD MADRID

▶ Begin the morning at **Plaza de la Villa** with its handsome 16th- and 17th-century palaces. Take the busy Calle Mayor as far as Calle de Felipe III, then turn into **Plaza Mayor** *(see pp22–3)*. Cross this magnificent square diagonally, leaving the ancient Calle Toledo, once the main exit route south from the city. On the way look out for the **Casa Hernanz** rope store *(see p113)* and other charming reminders that this was once an artisans' quarter. Looming on the left is the Baroque **Colegiata de San Isidro** *(see p112)*. Continue to La Latina metro.

Turn and follow **Plaza de la Cebada**, past the modern covered market. Turn right into **Plaza del Humilladero** and cross this square to the adjoining Plaza de San Andrés and its huge domed church. Straight ahead is a 16th-century palace, now the **Museo de los Orígenes (Casa de San Isidro)** *(see p107)*.

Follow the path round the back of the church into Costanilla de San Andrés, a narrow street which opens onto the historic **Plaza de la Paja**, a good area for bars and restaurants. On the corner of Calle de Alfonso VI is the **Colegio de San Ildefonso** whose students chant the results of the Christmas National Lottery in a distinctive sing-song.

By now you'll probably be ready for lunch. Vegetarians will be tempted by El Estragón *(Plaza de la Paja 10)*. Other good choices include the Basque Taberna Bilbao *(Calle Costanilla de San Andrés 8)* and Café Delic *(see p116)*.

See map on pp106–7 ←

The Best of the Rest

1 Ateneo de Madrid
MAP R5 ■ Calle del Prado 21 ■ Guided tours available, times vary (advance booking necessary) ■ Adm

One of Madrid's great cultural institutions, the Ateneo was founded in 1835 to promote the arts and sciences. The building contains a library of half a million volumes.

2 Colegiata de San Isidro
MAP M6 ■ Calle de Toledo 37 ■ Open for services

This imposing church was built in 1622 by the Jesuits. In 1768 the remains of Madrid's patron saint, San Isidro, were interred here.

3 Palacio de Santa Cruz
MAP M5 ■ Plaza de la Provincia 1

This 17th-century palace has lovely spired towers and interior court-yards. It was originally used as the city prison, but now houses the Ministry of Foreign Affairs.

Palacio de Santa Cruz

4 Teatro Español
MAP Q5 ■ Calle del Príncipe 25

Spain's National Theatre began as an open courtyard with a wooden plat-form for a stage. Look for medallions depicting the country's best-known dramatists above the entrance.

Previous pages Almudena Cathedral

5 Teatro de la Comedia
MAP Q5 ■ Calle del Príncipe 14

Despite its name, the Comedy Theatre stages classical plays. The lovely façade dates from 1874, while the auditorium was magnificently restored in the 1990s.

Tapas bar on Calle de las Huertas

6 Calle de las Huertas
MAP Q5

The name refers to the orchards that flourished here in the 17th century. Today the street is better known for its nightlife.

7 Muralla Árabe
MAP J5 ■ Cuesta de la Vega

Remains of the medieval defences are best seen from Parque Emir Mohammad I. The original section dates from the 9th century.

8 Cervecería Alemana
MAP P5 ■ Plaza de Sta Ana 6 ■ Closed Tue, Aug

This popular beer and *tapas* bar was founded in 1904 and is still going strong *(see p67)*.

9 Plaza de Tirso de Molina
MAP N6

Laid out in the 1840s, this square commemorates the infamous fictional seducer, Don Juan.

10 Cine Doré
MAP Q6 ■ Calle de Sta Isabel 3 ■ Closed Mon

The cinematograph was introduced to a Madrid audience from a booth on the site of what is now, fittingly, this cinema house *(see p64)*.

Specialist Shops

1 La Violeta
MAP Q4 ▪ Plaza de Canalejas 6

This quaint store, founded more than a century ago, sells its own brand of sugared violets, plus a small range of *marrons glacés*, pralines and other sweets.

2 Casa Hernanz
MAP M5 ▪ Calle de Toledo 18

One of a number of intriguing shops on Calle de Toledo, Casa Hernanz specializes in items made of rope, including woven baskets and mats, but especially its famous rope-soled espadrilles, available in every colour of the rainbow *(see p109)*.

3 Tea Shop
MAP M4 ▪ Calle Mayor 12

You will find an exquisite selection of teas from around the world in this delightful shop. Try the aromatic and exotic infusions such as "Andalusian Garden" or "La Siesta".

4 Casa de Diego
MAP P4 ▪ Puerta del Sol 12

The finest in handcrafted fans, exquisite scarves, veils, high-quality walking sticks and umbrellas. This is where Queen Letizia bought the fan for her wedding to King Felipe VI.

5 Biocentro
MAP P4 ▪ Calle de Espoz y Mina 3

Health food shop with a good selection of natural products, mainly food (including vacuum-packed 100 per cent veggie burgers) and cosmetics.

6 Casa Mira
MAP P4 ▪ Carrera de S Jerónimo 30

Founded in 1842 by Luis Mira, who knew how to cater for the famous Spanish sweet tooth, this *confitería* (confectioner) is best-known for its *turrón* (Christmas nougat), and also its marzipan, chocolate and *pestiños* (honey-coated pastries).

La Violeta sweets

7 Europa 20
MAP E4 ▪ Carrera de San Jerónimo 32

This family-run home furnishings store stocks a range of stylish modern furniture including sofas, lighting and well-designed accessories.

8 Guitarreria Manzanero
MAP C6 ▪ C/Santa Ana 12

Félix Manzanero is one of the finest guitar-makers in Spain, and his charming workshop displays part of his amazing collection of guitars and other musical instruments.

9 Jamones Julián Becerro
MAP L6 ▪ Cava Baja 41

This shop offers a variety of Iberian pork products from Salamanca, such as ham and sausages. Acorn ham (*jamón de bellota*) is considered to be the best. Cheese, foie gras and liqueurs are also sold.

Jamones Julián Becerro

10 Capas Seseña
MAP P4 ▪ Calle de la Cruz 23

Would-be matadors should first make their way here to be kitted out with the traditional Spanish cape. First established in 1901, this is still a family-run business where each cape is produced individually. Be warned, these celebrity favourites are not cheap *(see p72)*.

See map on pp106–7

Shops in La Latina

1 Caramelos Paco
MAP M5 ■ **Calle de Toledo 53–55**

The display windows of this famous sweet emporium are ablaze with colour. Some of the flavours – rice pudding, for example – may sound less appealing than others. To be fair to all, sugar-free sweets for diabetics are also created.

Caramelos Paco lolly

2 El Transformista
MAP C6 ■ **Calle de Mira el Río Baja 18**

Delve into this treasure trove of antique and second-hand furniture – everything from old mirrors and table lamps to painted plates and plastic chairs.

3 Casa Vega Alpargateria
MAP C5 ■ **Calle Toledo 57**

This Aladdin's cave sells an unusual array of goods ranging from saddles to espadrilles. Its interior seems to have changed little since it opened in 1860.

4 Fotocasion
MAP C6 ■ **Ribera de Curtidores 22**

Stocks just about everything the photographer might need – cameras (new and second-hand), film, camera cases, tripods and other specialist equipment. Also sells binoculars.

5 Mercado de la Cebada
MAP L6 ■ **Plaza Cebada 15**

If you want artisanal hams and cheeses but prefer not to go to a tourist spot, try this market. It is popular with locals, and many of its vendors supply some of Madrid's best restaurants (see p73).

6 María José Fermín
MAP C6 ■ **Ribera de Curtidores 9**

Wrought-iron enthusiasts, look no further. This family business deals in everything from coal scuttles and fire-guards to bellows, weather vanes and even milk churns.

7 Botería Julio Rodríguez
MAP C6 ■ **Calle del Águila 12**

One of the few remaining makers of authentic, superb quality wineskins, which make a fantastic souvenir of traditional Spain.

8 Nuevas Galerías
MAP C6 ■ **Ribera de Curtidores 12**

Shop at this gallery for prints, lithographs, repro-ceramics and antiques. Souvenir hunters should make a bee-line for Albarelo and Mercedes Cabeza de Vaca.

9 La Tienda de las Hamacas
MAP D6 ■ **Calle Miguel Servet 6**

This shop is dedicated to the fine art of making hammocks – La Tienda de las Hamacas sells every kind of hammock imaginable for the home or garden. Particularly special are the handmade Mayan styles.

La Tienda de las Hamacas

10 Kiki Market
MAP L6 ■ **Cava Alta 21**

Ideal for picking up tasty picnic goodies, this shop has a wide range of organic produce, including bread, cheese, ham, fruit and vegetables. It also has a great selection of olive oils and wines.

Nights Out

1 Casa Patas
MAP P6
Calle de
Cañizares 10
Enthusiasts rate
this attractive venue
as the best place for
traditional Spanish
flamenco acts.

2 Viva Madrid
MAP P6 Calle
Manuel Fernández y
González 7

Worth seeing for the
decorative tiles alone, this *tapas* bar
near Huertas really gets going after
10pm and is a popular hang-out with
the young crowd. In the summer you
may need to cool off on the terrace.
Becomes busy at weekends.

3 Café Central
MAP P5 Plaza del Ángel 10
Sophisticated jazz lovers enjoy this
Art Deco café at the top of Huertas.
There is a small admission charge,
depending on the artists.

4 Populart
MAP Q5 Calle de las
Huertas 22
Eclectic live music nightly – anything
from blues or jazz to Celtic – and
beer on tap. No cover charge, but
be warned that there's a steep mark-
up on drinks.

5 La Negra Tomasa
MAP P4 Corner of Calle
de Espoz y Mina, Cádiz 9
The live salsa music, performed from
Thursday to Saturday, is the main
draw of this noisy Cuban restaurant.

6 Candela
MAP P6 Calle Pelayo 48
A stalwart on the city's flamenco
scene for more than 30 years,
Candela is set in an atmospheric
vaulted cellar. Open nightly until
dawn, but the excellent flamenco
performances are held twice a week.

**Flamenco
dancer**

7 Teatro Circo Price
MAP E6 Ronda de
Atocha 35
This theatre is named after
an Irish horse tamer called
Thomas Price who came
to Madrid in the 19th
century and set up a
circus. It is now the best
place to see avant-garde
performances in Madrid.

8 Commo
MAP P5 Calle de
Espoz y Mina 22
This hip, lively club welcomes
dancers with its buzzing atmosphere.
It plays the *pachanga* style of
music and offers other varied
activities and inexpensive drinks.

Tablao Villa Rosa

9 Tablao Villa Rosa
MAP P5 Plaza de Santa
Ana 15
On a corner of bustling Plaza de
Santa Ana (see p109), this exquisitely
tiled restaurant offers polished and
entertaining flamenco performances,
combined with a choice of menus and
wine, twice every evening (see p51).

10 Berlín Cabaret 1930
MAP C5 Calle Costanilla de
San Pedro 11
With its cabaret interiors, this
venue hosts live shows with drag
queens, flamenco dancing and
cabaret performances. It's open
from Thursday to Saturday, with
music from the 1980s and 1990s.

See map on pp106–7

Places to Eat and Drink

1 Venta El Buscón
MAP P4 ▪ Calle Victoria 5
▪ 91 522 5412 ▪ €

Traditional *tapas* bar, decorated with paintings of the poet Quevedo. Serves incredible Spanish omelettes and fried squid, as well as local tapas *madrileñas*.

Café Delic's traditional dishes

2 Café Delic
MAP K6 ▪ Constanilla de San Andrés 14 ▪ 91 364 5450 ▪ €

This café features retro furnishings, some of which you can buy at its shop next door. It serves home-made quiches and salads at lunchtime and, in the evening, is a popular cocktail spot, due in part to its terrace on one of Madrid's prettiest squares.

3 Casa Lucas
MAP L6 ▪ Cava Baja 30 ▪ 91 365 0804 ▪ Closed Wed L ▪ €

Offers a good choice of wines and large *tapas* for sharing.

4 Casa Gonzalez
MAP Q5 ▪ Calle León 12 ▪ 91 429 5618 ▪ €

This popular wine bar is housed in a converted 1930s deli. There is a huge selection of wine, *empanadas* (pies) and ice cream.

5 Casa Lucio
MAP L6 ▪ Calle de la Cava Baja 35 ▪ 91 365 8217 ▪ Closed Aug ▪ €€

It's worth splashing out on a meal in this restaurant renowned for its roasts. Booking ahead is essential.

6 El Bonanno
MAP K6 ▪ Plaza del Humilladero 4 ▪ 91 366 6886 ▪ €

A Madrid classic, this popular bar is right in the heart of one of the city's liveliest nightlife districts. It draws an alternative, arty crowd, including musicians and actors, thanks to its relaxed vibe and well-priced drinks, including excellent *vermut*.

7 La Venencia
MAP Q5 ▪ Calle de Echegaray 7 ▪ 91 429 7313 ▪ €

Sherry is the speciality of this small, lively bar that serves simple *tapas*.

8 Alhambra
MAP P4 ▪ Calle de la Victoria 9 ▪ 91 521 0708 ▪ €

Enjoy good Spanish wine and Iberian ham at this atmospheric *tapas* bar. It is crowded at weekends (see p67).

9 Taberna Almendro 13
MAP L6 ▪ Calle del Almendro 13 ▪ 91 365 4252 ▪ €

This tastefully decorated *tapas* restaurant has an Andalusian theme.

10 The Roof
MAP P5 ▪ Hotel ME Madrid, Plaza Santa Ana 14 ▪ 91 701 6000 ▪ €€

This stylish rooftop terrace has two indoor bars, delicious cocktails and extraordinary views of the city.

Dramatic terrace of The Roof at night

Traditional Restaurants and Bars

PRICE CATEGORIES
For a three-course meal for one with half a bottle of wine (or equivalent meal), taxes and extra charges.

€ under €35 €€ €35–€70 €€€ over €70

1 La Posada de la Villa

MAP L6 ■ Calle de la Cava Baja 9 ■ 91 366 1860 ■ Closed Sun D, Aug ■ €€ ■ Dis. access

This attractive inn dates back to 1642. Traditional Castilian cooking is served, especially roasts.

2 Botín

MAP M5 ■ Calle de la Cuchilleros 17 ■ 91 366 4217 ■ €€

American writer Ernest Hemingway was a fan of this restaurant. His favourite dish, roast suckling pig, is still a house speciality *(see p70)*.

3 La Torre del Oro

MAP L4 ■ Plaza Mayor 26 ■ 91 366 5016 ■ €

Tapas are free when you buy a drink at this outrageous Andalusian bar, which is decorated with mounted bull heads, videos of bullfighting and gory pictures.

4 La Casa del Abuelo

MAP P4 ■ Calle de la Victoria 12 ■ 91 000 0133 ■ €

This *tapas* bar *par excellence* was founded in 1906 and is still going strong. The speciality of the house is prawns *(see p69)*.

5 Taberna Oliveros

MAP D6 ■ Calle San Millán 4 ■ 91 354 6252 ■ Closed Sun D, Mon, Jul, Aug ■ €

Dating back to 1857, this *taberna* has an old-world charm. It is worth trying the main speciality, *cocido madrileño* – a stew made from chickpeas, tripe and fried *bacalao* *(see p71)*.

6 Taberna de la Daniela

MAP M5 ■ Cuchilleros 9 ■ 91 366 2018 ■ €

Traditional cuisine, such as tapas and *cocido madrileño* (stew).

7 Casa Alberto

MAP Q5 ■ Calle de las Huertas 18 ■ 91 429 9356 ■ Closed Sun D, Mon, last 3 weeks of Aug ■ €

This historic tavern, where Cervantes wrote part of *Don Quixote*, serves traditional *madrileño* cooking.

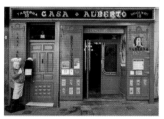

Casa Alberto

8 Taberna Maceiras

MAP R6 ■ Huertas 66 ■ 91 429 5818 ■ €

Chaotic and noisy, this restaurant is still well worth a visit for the great seafood, almond cake and wine.

9 Taberna de Antonio Sanchez

MAP N6 ■ Calle de Mesón de Paredes 13 ■ 91 539 7826 ■ Closed Sun D, 15–31 Aug ■ €

The ambience here is reason enough to visit this traditional inn. The delicious range of *tapas* includes black pudding with raisins *(see p68)*.

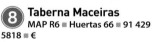

Taberna de Antonio Sanchez

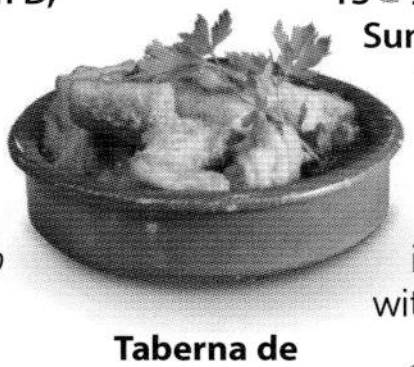

10 Prada a Tope

MAP E4 ■ Calle Principe 11 ■ 91 429 5921 ■ €€

Traditional classic dishes from the northern Spain region of Bierzo in Leon. Try the meat and the morcilla sausage which is spicy, but worth it.

See map on pp106–7

🔟 **Chueca and Malasaña**

Two of Madrid's most lively neighbourhoods lie just off the Gran Vía. Chueca was originally home to the city's blacksmiths and tile-makers. Run-down for many years, it enjoyed a renaissance after being adopted by Madrid's gay community – the area puts on its best clothes each summer for the Gay Pride celebrations. The 19th-century buildings around Plaza de Chueca have been given a new lease of life as trendy bars and restaurants. Neighbouring Malasaña was the focus of resistance against the French in 1808. Like Chueca, it became rather seedy, but is now a mainstay of Madrid nightlife.

Art Nouveau detail on Palacio Longoria

AREA MAP OF CHUECA AND MALASAÑA

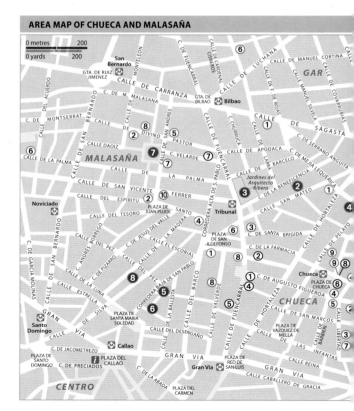

1 Casa de las Siete Chimeneas

MAP F3 ▪ Calle Infantas 31 ▪ Closed to the public

The "house of the seven chimneys" dates from around 1570 and is one of the best-preserved examples of domestic architecture in Madrid. It is said to be haunted by a former lover of Felipe II – not as far-fetched as it sounds, as a female skeleton was uncovered here at the end of the 19th century. The house belonged to Carlos III's chief minister, the Marqués de Esquilache, whose attempts to outlaw the traditional gentleman's cape and broad-brimmed hat, on the grounds that rogues used one to conceal weapons and the other to hide their faces, provoked a riot.

Museo del Romanticismo

2 Museo del Romanticismo

MAP E2 ▪ Calle de S Mateo 13 ▪ Open 9:30am–8:30pm Tue–Sat (Nov–Apr: 9:30am–6:30pm), 10am–3pm Sun & public hols ▪ Closed Mon, 1 & 6 Jan, 1 May, 24 Dec, 25 Dec, 31 Dec ▪ Adm (free Sat after 2pm)

This evocative museum recreates the Madrid of the Romantic era (c.1820–60), with rooms furnished in the style of the period. The real attraction lies in the ephemera: fans, figurines, dolls, old photograph albums, cigar cases and visiting cards. Among the paintings is a magnificent Goya in the chapel and a portrait of the Marqués de Vega-Inclán, whose personal possessions form the basis of the collection. The archetypal Spanish Romantic was Mariano José de Larra, a journalist with a caustic pen, who shot himself in 1837 after his lover ran off with another man. The pistol is one of the museum's prized exhibits.

3 Museo de Historia

MAP E2 ▪ Calle de Fuencarral 78 ▪ Open 10am–8pm Tue–Sun ▪ Closed Mon & public hols

Once a poorhouse, this museum traces the history of Madrid from the earliest times to the present day. Exhibits include mosaic fragments from a local Roman villa, pottery from the time of the Muslim occupation, a bust of Felipe II, and Goya's *Allegory of the City of Madrid*. The star attraction is a wooden model of the city constructed in 1830. Before leaving, note the elaborate Baroque portal, dating from the 1720s.

Palacio Longoria

4 Palacio Longoria
MAP E2 ▪ **Calle de Fernando VI, 4** ▪ **Closed to public**

The finest example of Art Nouveau architecture in Madrid was created for the banker Javier González Longoria in 1902. The architect was José Grases Riera, a disciple of Antoni Gaudí. Magnificently restored in the 1990s, the walls, windows and balconies are covered with luxuriant decoration suggesting plants, flowers and tree roots *(see p50)*.

5 Iglesia de San Antonio de los Alemanes
MAP N1 ▪ **Corredera Baja de S Pablo 16** ▪ **Open for services**

The entire surface area of this magnificent domed church is covered with lovely 17th-century frescoes depicting scenes from the life of St Anthony of Padua. The congregation included the sick and indigent residents of the adjoining hospice, who were allocated a daily ration of bread and boiled eggs. The church still has a soup kitchen, which feeds around 250 people a day.

6 triBall

MAP P2

The triBall district, delineated by Ballesta, Desengaño and Corredera Baja de San Pablo streets, was once one of the seediest areas in the city, before becoming popular with artists seeking inexpensive accommodation or work space. In recent years, the neighbourhood has been transformed almost beyond recognition: former bordellos are now vintage-style bars or boutiques (though few old-style taverns and groceries have withstood the wave of gentrification), and the prostitutes and drug-dealers have largely been replaced by hipsters.

7 Plaza del Dos de Mayo
MAP D2

This square in the heart of Malasaña commemorates the leaders of the insurrection of May 1808, Luis Daoíz and Pedro Velarde, who are buried at the Plaza de la Lealtad *(see p80)*. The site was chosen because, in those days, this was the artillery barracks of the Monteleón Palace, the main focus of resistance to the French. The brick arch now sheltering a sculpture of the two heroes was the entrance to the building. In the 1990s the square was taken over by under-age drinkers who gathered here at weekends for binges known as *botellón*. Though it has now been reclaimed by local residents, it is best avoided at night.

MANUELA MALASAÑA

The seamstress, who became a national heroine following the 1808 uprising, was still a teenager on that fateful day in May, when, so the story goes, she was approached by a couple of French soldiers. Despite her protestations, they insisted on conducting a body search, provoking her to stab at them with a pair of dressmaking scissors. They shot her dead, but her memory lives on in the district which now bears her name.

Plaza del Dos de Mayo

8 Iglesia San Plácido
MAP N1 ■ Calle S Roque 9
■ Open for services

Founded in 1622 by Don Jerónimo de Villanueva, a Madrid nobleman, in its early years this convent was darkened by scandal. Rumours of sexual misconduct among the novices led to an investigation by the Inquisition which implicated the chaplain, the abbess and the Don himself. It was even rumoured that Felipe IV made nocturnal visits here via a tunnel under the street.

9 Palacio de Justicia
MAP F2 ■ Plaza Villa de Paris ■ Closed to public

Designed by Francisco Carlier and Francisco Moradillo, and constructed between 1750 and 1757, the building served as a convent until 1870. The conversion into the Palace of Justice was carried out by architect Antonio Ruiz de Salces, but its present appearance is due to the restoration work that followed a fire in 1915.

Iglesia de Santa Bárbara

10 Iglesia de Santa Bárbara
MAP F3 ■ Calle de General Castaños 2 ■ Open for services

The monastery of the Royal Salesians was founded by Bárbara de Braganza, the wife of Ferdinand VI, as a refuge from her overbearing mother-in-law should the king die before her (in fact, she died first). The lavish Baroque church (1750) by Francisco Gutiérrez features the tombs of Fernando VI and his wife.

AN AFTERNOON OF CULTURE AND CAFÉS

▶ Begin with a pre-lunch *vermut* at the traditional **Bodega Ángel Sierra** *(Plaza Chueca 11, 91 531 0126)* and then head into the nearby **Mercado de San Antón**. Admire the market's fabulous range of produce, then enjoy lunch on its rooftop terrace, **La Cocina de San Antón** *(91 330 0294)*.

After lunch, check out the outlet shoe stores along the **Calle Augusto Figueroa** and the boutiques on **Calle Fuencarral** (Basque fashion label Hoss Intropia is at no. 16, and Barcelona design firm Custo is at no.29). At the top of the street, you'll find the excellent **Museo de Historia** *(see p119)*.

After visiting the museum, stroll along **Calle de San Vicente Ferrer**, where you'll find some of the city's few surviving tiled shop-fronts from the 1920s (including a pharmacy at the corner of Calle de San Andrés), and make for the **Plaza Dos de Mayo**, the historic heart of the Malasaña district. At the corner of the square, **Pepe Botella** *(Calle de San Andrés 12, 91 522 43 09)*, a shabby-chic favourite of artists and actors, is the perfect spot for a break.

Continue east to the **Centro Cultural Conde Duque** *(see p62)*, a former barracks which has been converted into an excellent cultural centre, and is home to the city's collection of contemporary art. After visiting the gallery, walk to the nearby **Plaza de los Comendadores**, where you can join the locals at one of the terrace cafés, such as Federal at no. 9 *(91 532 8424)*.

See map on pp118–19

Fashion Shops

Leather bags and other accessories for sale at Salvador Bachiller

① Camper
MAP P1 ■ Calle Fuencarral 42 (Cnr Augusto Figueroa)
For internationally acclaimed, comfortable and casual footwear, head to Camper, which stocks a selection of shoes produced in Mallorca.

② Lotta Vintage
MAP E3 ■ Hernán Cortés 9
The perfect shop for vintage fashion, this store offers an exquisite selection of clothes and accessories from the 1950s, '60s, '70s and '80s.

③ Mott
MAP E3 ■ Barquillo 31
Find original outfits and accessories from a range of worldwide designers at this lovely boutique. Caters for both men and women.

④ Desigual
MAP P2 ■ Calle de Fuencarral 36
This Spanish brand, hailing from Barcelona, has been taking Europe by storm in recent years. Offers funky, colourful street fashions.

⑤ Custo Barcelona
MAP P2 ■ Calle de Fuencarral 29
Set up by Custo and David Dalmau in the early 1980s, this fashion house is inspired by the colours and patterns of California. The shop has plenty of pretty dresses and coats for women, while style-conscious men will love the graphic T-shirts and tailored jackets.

⑥ L'Habilleur
MAP E3 ■ Plaza de Chueca 8
At L'Habilleur you can pick up last season's designer clothes at a fraction of the original prices.

⑦ La Mona Checa
MAP D2 ■ Calle Velarde 2
This charming shop is packed with a great selection of vintage clothing and accessories. The shop also has an area for art displays, and a collection of old film cameras.

⑧ Salvador Bachiller
MAP E3 ■ Gravina 11
Since 1978, this well established Spanish designer has been producing excellent leather goods, which include bags, purses, wallets and suitcases. Find his designs at reasonable rates at this outlet.

⑨ Fariña & Almuzara
MAP E4 ■ Calle de Conde de Xiquena 12
Beautiful hand-crafted jewellery is made on the premises from stones such as amber and amethyst. There is a range of styles, and you can design your own piece.

Alcoba bag

⑩ Alcoba
MAP E3 ■ Calle de Argensola 2
This small outlet sells a great range of glitzy evening wear, with sequinned bags, scarves and jewellery and other accessories, as well as candles and picture frames.

Specialist Shops

1 Patrimonio Comunal Olivarero

MAP E2 ■ Calle de Mejía Lequerica 1
Spain produces more olive oil than any other country, and this supplier stocks the finest Extra Virgin varieties. Also look for the DO *(denominación de origen)* quality control on the label.

2 Antigua Casa Crespo

MAP D2 ■ Calle Divino Pastor 29
This charming sandal shop was established in 1863. It specializes in traditional espadrilles, hand-woven and sewn by artisans from the La Rioja region of Spain. The shop is often patronized by Spanish royalty.

Candle from Velas de la Ballena

3 Reserva y Cata
MAP F3 ■ Calle de Conde de Xiquena 13
If you are interested in Iberian wines, take care not to overlook this basement merchant with its excellent selection of Spanish wines and liqueurs. Tastings are also on offer.

Reserva y Cata

4 Templo de Susu

MAP D2 ■ Calle del Espíritu Santo 1
The oldest vintage clothing store on the street, this shop offers good quality, reasonably-priced second-hand treasures for men and women.

5 Kantharos

MAP E3 ■ Divino Pastor 6
Stylish gifts at this shop include pocket- as well as wrist-watches, keyrings, jewellery and ink wells.

6 Tipos Infames
MAP D3 ■ Calle San Joaquin 3
A modern, inviting bookshop with an interesting and eclectic selection of titles. The walls here are hung with changing art exhibitions, and the bookshop even has its own wine bar.

7 Almirante 23
MAP F3 ■ Calle del Almirante 23
If it's collectable, this shop collects it – postcards, perfume containers, tobacco tins, cameras, sunglasses, cinema programmes, menus and cigarette cards. You will find it difficult to drag yourself away.

8 Velas de la Ballena
MAP P1 ■ Calle Fuencarral 47
Candles in every size and shape are arranged in rainbow colours in this small shop. It also has incense and incense burners, lanterns and candles for patios and gardens.

9 Mad is Mad
MAP Q1 ■ Calle Pelayo 48
This tiny Chueca art gallery showcases the work of up-and-coming local artists in a wide range of media, from photography to illustration. The interesting exhibitions are always worth a look, and could provide you with an original and affordable souvenir.

10 Alice in Wonderland
MAP F3 ■ Calle Tamayo y Baus 7
For some serious pampering, head to this wonderland of indulgence. This friendly, retro basement shop also offers manicures, pedicures and other beauty treatments.

See map on pp118–19

Places to Eat and Drink

1 La Manduca de Azagra

MAP E2 ■ Calle Sagasta 14 ■ 91 591 0112 ■ Closed Sun & public hols, Aug ■ €€€

This *Navarre* restaurant with its striking avant-garde decor is famed for its perfect

Fish dish at La Manduca de Azagra

vegetables, fresh fish and grilled meats such as rack of lamb. Tapas are served at the bar.

2 Arce

MAP Q1 ■ Calle Augusto Figueroa 32 ■ 91 522 0440 ■ Closed Sun, Mon, Easter Sat & Sun ■ €€€

Chueca's top restaurant is not cheap, but it is an absolute gem. The menu changes regularly to make the most of seasonal produce.

3 Ribeira do Miño

MAP E3 ■ Calle Santa Brígida 1 ■ 91 521 9854 ■ Closed Mon, Aug ■ €€

This back-street Galician *marisquería* is well-known for its good value shellfish, fresh fish and delicious *Crêpes Suzette*.

4 El Cisne Azul

MAP R1 ■ Calle Gravina 19 ■ 91 521 3799 ■ €€€

Exquisite large tapas are on the menu here. Try the wild mushrooms, rocket salad, lamb chops and steaks.

5 Sergi Arola Gastro

MAP F1 ■ Zurbano 31 ■ 91 310 2169 ■ Closed Sun & Mon ■ Dis. access ■ €€€

Renowned chef Sergi Arola creates imaginative and exotic dishes at this elegant, Michelin-starred restaurant.

6 Sala Clamores

MAP D1 ■ Calle de Alburquerque 14 ■ 91 445 5480 ■ €

Enjoy live jazz, blues, or tango performances by renowned artists along with a cocktail at this large jazz club.

7 Pepe Botella

MAP D2 ■ Calle S Andrés 12 ■ 91 522 4309 ■ €

Relax and people-watch while having a coffee, beer or glass of wine at this old café with its comfortable velvet banquettes and marble-topped tables.

8 Fábrica Maravillas

MAP P1 ■ Valverde 29 ■ 91 521 8753 ■ €

This modern space, with its own brewhouse, offers a number of different types of craft beer on tap. From blonde ale to the most intense, dark Imperial Stout, each has its own personal touch.

9 La Kitchen

MAP F3 ■ Calle Prim 5 ■ 91 360 4974 ■ Closed Sun & public hols ■ €€

This bright restaurant serves Spanish dishes with a modern twist. It is essential to book a table.

Vaulted interior of La Kitchen

10 Café Manuela

MAP D2 ■ Calle de S Vicente Ferrer 29 ■ 91 531 7037 ■ €

More like a club for young people who drop in to chat, read the paper or to play board games. Draught beer, cocktails and snacks are served.

Tabernas

PRICE CATEGORIES
For a three-course meal for one with half
a bottle of wine (or equivalent meal),
taxes and extra charges.
....
€ under €35 €€ €35–€70 €€€ over €70

1 La Ardosa
MAP F3 ▪ Calle de Colón 13
▪ 91 521 4979 ▪ €

This cosy *taberna* serves Guinness on
tap, as well as excellent tapas. Try the
fabada (bean and squid stew) *(see p66)*.

2 La Taberna la Lirio
MAP D2 ▪ Calle del Espíritu
Santo 30 ▪ 91 521 3958 ▪ €

Literary quotes line the brick walls of
this bar. Serves delicious traditional
Andalucian tapas with a modern twist.

3 Libertad 8
MAP F3 ▪ Calle Libertad 8
▪ 91 532 1150 ▪ €

Relax at this Bohemian café-bar and
listen to the singer-songwriters who
perform in the back room.

4 El Comunista
MAP E2 ▪ Calle de Augusto
Figueroa 35 ▪ 91 521 7012 ▪ Closed
Sun, Mon D ▪ €

One of the most authentic *tabernas*
in the city, El Comunista offers
simple home cooking.

5 La Trastienda
MAP R1 ▪ Augusto Figueroa 24
▪ 91 330 0271 ▪ €€

Located within the San Antón
market, this bar serves Basque
specialities, and at least 12 varieties
of creamy croquettes.

6 Bodegas el Maño
MAP D2 ▪ Calle de la Palma 64
▪ 91 521 5057 ▪ Closed Sun D ▪ €

This old-fashioned wine cellar really
looks the part, with fluted columns
and painted barrels. There's draught
vermouth, beer and wine, and a
good range of tapas – the stuffed
squid is delicious.

El Bocaíto

7 El Bocaíto
MAP E3 ▪ Calle de la Libertad
6 ▪ 91 532 1219 ▪ Closed Sun, Aug
▪ €

Classic tapas. The prawn and garlic
tostadas are wonderful *(see p69)*.

8 Café Isadora
MAP E3 ▪ Divino Pastor 14
▪ 91 445 7154 ▪ €

This stylish bar is decorated with
posters of the legendary dancer,
Isadora Duncan. Jazz plays in the
background while you chat over
champagne cocktails and unusual
liqueur coffees.

9 Taberna Ángel Sierra
MAP R1 ▪ Calle Gravina 11
▪ 91 531 0126 ▪ Closed Wed, 2 weeks
in Aug ▪ €

Try the *escabeche de atún* (pickled
tuna) at this tapas bar, which has
vermouth on tap.

**10 Cervecería Santa
Bárbara**
MAP E2 ▪ Plaza de S Bárbara 8
▪ 91 319 0449 ▪ €

Large modern bar, popular with
office workers, serving beer on tap.
Good range of tapas *(see p67)*.

Cervecería Santa Bárbara

See map on pp118–19

TOP 10 Comunidad de Madrid

Aranjuez fountain

The Comunidad de Madrid is a vast region covering 8,000 sq km (3,000 sq miles), with a population now exceeding five million. To the north of the capital is the Sierra de Guadarrama, a majestic mountain range, stretching more than 100 km (60 miles) east–west. Visitors to El Escorial, Valle de los Caídos, or Manzanares el Real will enjoy the superb views as well as the fresh mountain air. An excursion to the university town of Alcalá de Henares can easily be combined with Chinchón. Alternatively you could couple the latter with the fascinating walled city of Toledo, or with Aranjuez, an oasis of gardens and orchards in an otherwise parched landscape.

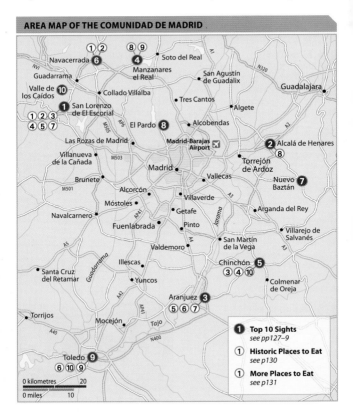

AREA MAP OF THE COMUNIDAD DE MADRID

1 **Top 10 Sights**
see pp127–9

1 **Historic Places to Eat**
see p130

1 **More Places to Eat**
see p131

0 kilometres 20

0 miles 10

Magnificent El Escorial

1 El Escorial

Apart from the famous monastery and the views of the Sierra, the attractions of El Escorial include the magnificent Coliseo, dating from 1771, and the two royal lodges *(see pp40–43)*.

2 Alcalá de Henares

MAP B1 ■ Train from Atocha ■ University: Open for tours 10am–2pm, 4–8pm Mon–Fri, 10am–3pm, 4–8pm Sat, Sun & public hols ■ Adm

This historic town has been designated a UNESCO World Heritage Site due to its wealth of splendid Renaissance and Baroque architecture. It was also the birthplace of Miguel de Cervantes, author of *Don Quixote*, and also of the ill-fated Queen of England, Catherine of Aragon, the first wife of Henry VIII. The town's importance dates from the late 15th century when the head of the Spanish church, Cardinal Cisneros, founded a university here. A tour of the buildings, including the main hall with its *mudéjar* ceiling, is a must. Also worth seeing is Teatro Cervantes, the oldest public theatre in Europe, founded in the 17th century and restored in the 1990s.

3 Aranjuez

MAP B1 ■ Train from Atocha or themed Tren de la Fresa *(see p59)* ■ Palacio Real: Open Apr–Sep: 10am–8pm Tue–Sun; Oct–Mar: 10am–6pm Tue–Sun (gardens open 8am–sunset) ■ Closed 24 Dec, 25 Dec, 31 Dec ■ Adm (free for EU citizens Apr–Sep: 5–8pm Wed & Thu; Oct–Mar: 3–6pm Wed & Thu)

This gem of a town, a UNESCO World Heritage Site, should not be missed. The Palacio Real, summer residence of Spain's Bourbon rulers, is sumptuously decorated in the French style. No expense was spared either on the extravagant folly known as the Casa del Labrador, in the grounds near the River Tagus. The town has preserved some *corralas* – balconied wooden dwellings, built around a courtyard. The Mercado de Abastos is a good source for picnic provisions, and local strawberries, sold at roadside stalls, make the perfect dessert. The town is also famous for its asparagus.

4 Manzanares el Real

MAP B1 ■ Bus no. 724 from Plaza de Castilla ■ Castle: Open Oct–May 10am–5:30pm Tue–Fri, 10am–6pm Sat & Sun. Garden: Jun–Sep: 10am–5:30pm Tue–Fri, 10am–6pm Sat & Sun; Oct–Mar: 10am–7pm Tue–Thu, Sun & hols, 10am–midnight Fri & Sat ■ Closed Mon & public hols ■ Adm

This Sierra town is dominated by its well-preserved 15th-century castle. Almost as ancient is the church of Nuestra Señora de las Nieves (Our Lady of the Snows) with its 30-m (100-ft) high belltower. Hikers will enjoy the La Pedriza regional park with its massive granite boulders.

Manzanares el Real castle

Bullfighting in Chinchón Plaza Mayor

5 Chinchón

MAP B1 ■ **Bus La Veloz no. 337 from Plaza Conde Casal**

Life in this attractive little town revolves around the Plaza Mayor, the galleried main square, dating from the 16th century. Originally a cattle market, the square is the focus of a Holy Week procession on Good Friday, a passion play on Easter Saturday and bullfights in July and August. While you're here, it's worth trying the local speciality, *anís*, a liquorice-flavoured liqueur (ask for "Chinchón"). Also worth seeing is the Iglesia de la Asunción, with a painting of the *Assumption of the Virgin* by Goya, whose brother was the local priest.

6 Navacerrada

MAP B1 ■ **Bus 691 from Moncloa**

At 1,860 m (6,100 ft), Navacerrada is the gateway to the Sierra de Guadarrama. Ski enthusiasts head straight for the Navacerrada Pass (Puerto de Navacerrada), but the town itself should not be overlooked. As well as the parish church, which has an impressive 15th-century tower, and the 16th-century Church of the Nativity, the craft shops are worth a browse. Cafés abound on Plaza Mayor and there are hiking trails in the surrounding forests.

7 Nuevo Baztán

MAP B1 ■ **Road: M-219 and R-3**

This settlement south of Alcalá de Henares was the brainchild of an 18th-century nobleman from Navarre, Juan de Goyeneche. Goyeneche built the estate so that he could supervise his various industrial enterprises, which were among the most advanced of the day. The Baroque palace, the domed church of St Francis Xavier and the workers' houses, which were designed by José de Churriguera himself, are the main attractions.

8 El Pardo

MAP B1 ■ **Bus No. 601 from Moncloa** ■ **Palacio del Pardo: Open daily Apr–Sep: 10am–8pm; Oct–Mar: 10am–6pm** ■ **Adm (free for EU citizens Apr–Sep: 5–8pm Wed & Thu; Oct–Mar: 3–6pm Wed & Thu)**

El Pardo is now a suburb of Madrid but was in open countryside when Enrico III built a hunting lodge here in the early 15th century. The Palacio Real de El Pardo was built by the Bourbons and substantially enlarged during the reign of Carlos III. More recently it was the official residence of General Franco, and it is now where visiting heads of state stay. The tapestries, from sketches by Goya, are the outstanding feature.

Royal palace of El Pardo

TREN DE CERVANTES

The Cervantes train is an enjoyable way to see the sights of Alcalá de Henares *(see p127)*. During the pleasant 25-minute journey, hostesses in period costume hand out cakes and snacks, and help visitors. On arrival there is a welcome by musicians, followed by a tour of the old quarter, including the university. Some local restaurants offer discounts to train travellers.

The alcázar of Toledo

⑨ Toledo
Road A42 (72km); RENFE train from Atocha Station ■ www.toledo-turismo.com

Just 30 minutes by express train from Madrid, Toledo is a beautiful walled city with an alcázar crowning a hilltop overlooking the Tagus River. It is known as the "city of three cultures", and Christians, Muslims and Jews co-existed peacefully here for centuries. Toledo's most famous resident was El Greco, who never tired of painting the city's skyline. Some of his works are on display in the Casa-Museo El Greco but his most famous painting, *The Burial of the Count of Orgaz* (1588), is displayed in the Iglesia de Santo Tomé. The Sinagoga del Tránsito, which contains the Museo Sefardí, was built in the 13th century, and is a jewel of Mudéjar architecture.

⑩ Valle de los Caídos
MAP B1 ■ Road A-6 north, exit (salida) at M-600 ■ The valley is closed indefinitely to visitors ■ The Basílica still opens for worship between 10am and 7pm

The "Valley of the Fallen" was General Franco's memorial to his war dead from the Spanish Civil War (1936–9). The crypt and basílica, cut into the mountainside, were built by prison labourers. The valley's most striking feature is a cross, 152-m (500-ft) high and 56-m (180-ft) wide. Franco is buried in the crypt.

Valle de los Caídos cross

A DAY IN MANZANARES

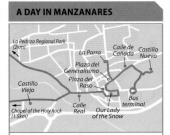

▶ **MORNING**

To reach **Manzanares**, take bus No. 721 from Plaza de Castilla, alighting at Avenida de Madrid. There's a supermarket near the bus stop if you want to stock up for a picnic. Take Calle del Castillo as far as **Calle de Cañada** and the restored 15th-century castle, from where there are good views of the storks fishing in the reservoir. Return along Calle de Cañada to the old town square, **Plaza del Generalísimo**, where you'll find several good cafés and bars if you are ready for a coffee and a rest.

Cross the tree-sheltered Plaza del Raso, passing a small cemetery, and you'll reach the 16th-century Church of Our Lady of the Snows with its elegant Renaissance portico. Walk around the church for more views of the lake. Return to **Plaza del Raso** and take **Calle Real**, crossing the River Manzanares to the ruins of the old castle *(castillo viejo)*. Then follow the river to the Chapel of the Holy Rock *(Ermita de la Peña Sacra)*, built on a huge granite slab. Every Whitsun a procession in honour of the Virgin makes its way here from the cemetery.

Head to the Plaza del Sagrado Corazón and then stroll up to Calle Panaderos for a hearty lunch at **La Parra** *(see p130)*.

AFTERNOON

Spend a leisurely afternoon enjoying the invigorating, fresh mountain air and splendid vistas of **La Pedriza** regional park.

See map on p126 ←

Historic Places to Eat

El Charolés
MAP A1 ■ Calle de Floridablanca 24, San Lorenzo de El Escorial ■ 91 890 5975 ■ €€

At what is considered to be the best restaurant in town, chef Manuel Miguez makes his renowned *cocido madrileño* (the classic, meaty Madrid stew) on Wednesdays. There is a summer terrace.

2 Las Viandas
MAP A1 ■ Plaza Constitución 2, San Lorenzo de El Escorial ■ 91 890 0986 ■ €€

This restaurant serves very good, seasonal food. There is a small, summer terrace where you can enjoy a drink before your meal.

3 Fonda Genara
MAP A1 ■ Plaza S Lorenzo 2, El Escorial ■ 91 890 1636 ■ Closed Tue (summer) ■ €

In an 18th-century building with theatre memorabilia, this restaurant has Castilian dishes, such as *rabo de toro* (oxtail). Set-price menu.

4 Horizontal
MAP A1 ■ Camino Horizontal, El Escorial ■ 91 890 3811 ■ Closed Mon–Wed D in winter ■ €€

This classy restaurant has wonderful vistas of the sierra – book a terrace table in summer. It serves first-class international cuisine.

5 Parrilla Príncipe
MAP A1 ■ Calle Mariano Benebente 12, San Lorenzo de El Escorial ■ 91 890 1548 ■ Closed Tue, 15–28 Feb ■ €

Grilled fish is the speciality of this hotel-restaurant based in an 18th-century palace.

6 Locum
C/Locum 6, Toledo ■ 92 522 3235 ■ Closed Sun D ■ €€

Tables are set on wooden galleries around the internal courtyard of this elegant 18th-century townhouse. The cuisine – classic local dishes with some contemporary options – is lauded as some of the best in Toledo.

7 Croché Cafetín
MAP A1 ■ Calle San Lorenzo 6, San Lorenzo de El Escorial ■ 91 890 5282 ■ €

Step back in time as you enter this Art Nouveau interior that boasts a handsome wooden bar counter, red velvet booths and aproned waiters.

8 La Parra
MAP B1 ■ Calle Panaderos 15, Manzanares El Real ■ 91 853 9577 ■ Closed Mon, 21 Aug–12 Sep ■ €

This traditional restaurant serves heart-warming country fare, such as stew made with beans and hare *(fabes con liebre)* and roast kid *(cabrito asado)*.

Traditional dining at La Parra

9 Rincón del Alba
MAP A1 ■ Calle Paloma 2, Manzanares El Real ■ 91 853 9111 ■ €€

Delectable fish and shellfish dishes, plus views of the Santillana marsh and La Pedriza mountain range.

10 Adolfo
C/Hombre de Palo 7, Toledo ■ 92 522 7321 ■ Closed Sun D ■ €€

Enjoy updated versions of traditional local recipes in an attractive dining room with beams and deep-red walls.

More Places to Eat

PRICE CATEGORIES

For a three-course meal for one with half
a bottle of wine (or equivalent meal),
taxes and extra charges.

€ under €35 ■ €€ €35–€70 ■ €€€ over €70

1 Terraza Jardín Felipe

MAP A1 ■ Calle Mayo 2,
Navacerrada ■ 91 853 1041 ■ Closed
Tue, Sun–Thu D (winter) ■ €

This restaurant in a stone farmhouse
is worth seeking out. Chef Felipe del
Olmo is known for his stylish cooking
– try the grilled hake in a delicious
squid sauce. During the summer
ask for a table on the large terrace.

2 Las Postas

MAP A1 ■ Road M-601, 10.2
km, Navacerrada ■ 91 856 02 50 ■ €€

This roadside hotel-restaurant serves
Castilian meat dishes in an attractive
dining room, the centrepiece of which
is a 16th-century retablo. You can also
enjoy live music on Saturday nights.

3 La Balconada

MAP B2 ■ Plaza Mayor,
Chinchón ■ 91 894 1303 ■ Closed
Wed ■ €€

Ideally situated, "the balcony" overlooks Chinchón's main square. It
serves typical Castilian fare such as
sopa de ajo (garlic soup), menestra
(lamb and vegetable stew) and
pepitoria de gallina (chicken in an
almond and egg sauce).

4 Mesón de la Virreina

MAP B2 ■ Plaza Mayor 28,
Chinchón ■ 91 894 0015 ■ €€

This atmospheric restaurant serves
Castilian dishes. Ask for a window or
balcony table on an upper floor.

5 Casa José

MAP B2 ■ Calle Abastos 32,
Aranjuez ■ 91 891 1488 ■ Closed Sun
D, Mon, Aug ■ €€€

The cuisine at this Michelin-starred
restaurant is based on home-grown
produce. Try the tasting menu.

6 Casa Pablo

MAP B2 ■ Calle Almíbar 42,
Aranjuez ■ 91 891 1451 ■ Closed
second week Jan, 1–15 Aug ■ €€

This cosy restaurant has the feel of
an old tavern. Meat and fresh fish
are the specialities.

7 El Castillo 1806

MAP B2 ■ Reales Jardines del
Príncipe, Aranjuez ■ 91 891 3000
■ Closed Mon ■ €€

Located in the grounds of Casa del
Labrador, the house speciality here
is cordero al sarmiento (grilled lamb).

8 Hostería del Estudiante

MAP B1 ■ Calle Colegios 8,
Alcalá de Henares ■ 91 888 0330
■ Closed Sun–Tue (winter) ■ €€

Part of the Parador Hotel, a speciality
here is the migas castellanas (breadcrumbs in garlic with fried eggs).

9 La Mar Salá

C/Honda 9, Toledo ■ 92 525
4785 ■ Closed Sun, Tue Wed D, Mon
■ €€

This small, romantic restaurant,
tucked away on the edge of Toledo's
historic quarter, specializes in seafood. Imaginative cuisine, such as
grilled octopus with pistachio alioli.

10 Mesón Cuevas del Vino

MAP B2 ■ Calle de Benito
Hortelano 13, Chinchón ■ 91 894
0206 ■ Closed Sun D ■ €

This old olive-oil mill and wine cellar
offers an authentic taste of Spain
with traditional sierra cooking.

Mesón Cuevas del Vino

See map on p126

Streetsmart

Café tables, Plaza Mayor

Getting To And Around Madrid

Arriving by Air

Madrid's international airport, the Aeropuerto **Adolfo Suárez Madrid-Barajas**, is 12 kilometres (7 miles) east of the city.

There are four terminals: Terminals 1, 2 and 3 for Air Europa, Ryanair, easyJet and other members of Star Alliance and SkyTeam; and Terminal 4 for Iberia and Oneworld Alliance flights. T4 is accessible via free shuttle buses that leave from the other terminals. If your departure gate is in T4S, check-in at T4 and take the automatic train to the T4S building. Facilities include banks, hotel and rail reservation services, pharmacies, tourist information, left-luggage, post office, shops, places to eat and car hire.

The Línea Exprés airport bus operates 24 hours a day and departs regularly from outside T1, T2 and T4 to Atocha-renfe train station in the city centre (journey time around 40 minutes). City bus no. 200 runs from 5:30am to 11pm from T1, T2, T3 and T4 to the Avenida de América transport hub. Taxis take at least 30 minutes. The Barajas metro link (line 8) from T2 and T4 takes 12 minutes to Nuevos Ministerios, and the Cercanías (overground) train runs from T4 to Madrid's main stations.

Madrid's airport is served by all the major national and international airlines. There are regular flights within Spain with Vueling, Air Europa and Ryanair, while Iberia operates a shuttle service between Barcelona and Madrid with up to 30 flights a day. British Airways and Iberia are the main carriers from London Heathrow and London City, while there are flights with easyJet, Ryanair, Norwegian Air and Air Europa from Dublin, Liverpool, London Luton, London Gatwick, London Stansted, Bristol, Edinburgh and Manchester.

There are also direct flights from national and low-cost airlines to most major European cities. From the US, American Airlines flies direct from New York, Miami and Dallas/Fort Worth, **Delta** flies direct from New York and Atlanta, Iberia flies direct from New York, Miami and Chicago. Qantas flies to Madrid from Australia and New Zealand via Dubai and other stopovers.

Arriving by Train

You can travel direct from France or Portugal. The national Spanish rail operator is **renfe**. Madrid's main stations are Estación de Atocha in the south and Estación de Chamartín in the north. Both are connected via the metro. Buy tickets from stations or travel agents, or book over the telephone or through the renfe website.

Atocha serves trains from southern Spain and Portugal. The AVE terminal handles the trains to Seville, Málaga, Toledo, Barcelona, Valencia, Zaragoza, Huesca, Albacete, Cordoba and Cuenca. The station has exchange facilities and shops.

Chamartín serves trains from northwest Spain. The AVE train serves Madrid–Segovia–Valladolid, Palencia y León. Facilities here include money exchange, cafés, car hire, post office, tourist information, hotel reservations and a shopping centre.

Arriving by Bus

There are three main bus and coach stations in Madrid. The largest and most important of these is the **Estación de Méndez Álvaro**, which is where travellers from France, Portugal and many of Spain's major cities arrive. The **Estación de Avenida** de América is used mainly for services to towns and cities within the Comunidad de Madrid, and the smaller **Estación de Conde de Casal** provides services to a handful of major Spanish cities, as well as to Portugal.

Arriving by Car

You need two days to drive from the UK, either via the cross-Channel ferry or the Channel tunnel. A third option is the ferry to Bilbao or Santander, followed by a four-hour drive from Bilbao or a five-hour drive from Santander. Roads are good, but expect heavy traffic on the outskirts of Madrid. Madrid is linked to the rest of Spain and Europe by autopistas (toll highways) and toll-free roads.

Getting Around by Metro and Train

Metro trains run from 6am to 1:30am. The 12 lines are colour-coded but you need to know your direction of travel and the name of the end station. Renfe runs suburban rail services *(cercanías)* to towns around the city. The train service is connected at several points with the metro.

Getting Around by Bus

Buses run 365 days a year, 24 hours a day. Bus route maps can be obtained from tourist offices *(see p139)*. Night buses known as *buhos* (owls) depart from Plaza de Cibeles and run every 20 to 35 minutes. Metrobus tickets are valid.

Getting Around by Taxi

City taxis are white with a diagonal red stripe and a green light on the roof. They may be hailed or hired at a taxi rank or by phone. Extra charges apply on Sundays, public holidays and at night. If you order a taxi by phone, the meter starts running from the moment the taxi arrives at your location.

Getting Around on Foot

The historic centre is relatively compact and easy to explore on foot.

Getting Around by Car

Driving in central Madrid, with its narrow streets and restricted on-street parking, is not recommended.

If you choose to drive, use an official underground car park or designated pay-and-display area – green or blue lines indicate a limit of one or two hours. Illegally parked cars may be impounded and should be collected as soon as possible, since fines rise every hour.

Getting Around on Two Wheels

Madrid is not a bicycle-friendly city, and has very few dedicated cycle lanes, although this is slowly improving. The city has introduced a bike-sharing system (electric ones, due to the steep city streets), **BiciMAD**, which has some 130 hire stations dotted around the city centre. Crash helmets must be worn on mopeds and motorcycles. Numerous companies provide moped rental, including **Cooltra**.

Tickets and Travelcards

A Metrobus ticket, valid for 10 journeys, is the most economical way of getting around the city and costs €12.20. You must stamp your ticket at the beginning of each journey. The Tourist Travel Pass is valid for up to 7 days and allows unlimited travel on all public transport. Tickets and travel passes are available from metro stations, *estancos* (tobacconists) and newspaper kiosks. Single metro tickets are sold in the station and cost €1.50. Note that there is a supplement for metro journeys to and from the airport.

DIRECTORY

AIRPORT

Barajas Airport
(91 393 6000
w aena.es

TRAIN

renfe
(902 320 320
(24 hours)
w renfe.com

BUS

EMT (local buses)
(91 406 88 10
w emtmadrid.es

Estación de Avenida de América
(902 42 22 42

Estación de Conde de Casal
(90 244 4403

Estación de - Méndez Álvaro
(91 468 42 00
w estaciondeautobuses.com

Eurolines
(91 506 3360
w eurolines.es

Metro Madrid (METRO)
(91 779 6399
w metromadrid.es

TAXI

Radio Taxi
(91 447 32 32

Tele Taxi
(91 371 21 31

CAR RENTAL

Avis
(902 180 854
w avis.es

Budget
(902 112 585
w budget.es

Hertz
(902 402 405
w hertz.es

TWO-WHEEL RENTAL

BiciMAD
(010, 91 529 8210
w bicimad.com

Cooltra
(91 299 44 94
w cooltra.com/Madrid

Practical Information

Passports and Visas

No visa is required for citizens of EU countries, the United States, Canada, Australia, Iceland, Norway or Switzerland, who are planning to stay for less than 90 days. Passports need to be valid for three months beyond the end of your stay. Citizens of other countries should consult their Spanish embassy or consulate for information before travelling.

Customs Regulations and Immigration

For EU citizens there are no limits on goods that can be taken into or out of Spain, provided they are for your personal use. If you are coming from outside the EU, you may import the following allowances duty-free: 200 cigarettes or equivalent in tobacco; 1 litre of spirits (exceeding 22 per cent proof) and 2 litres of wine; 50ml of perfume and 250ml of eau de toilette; plus gifts up to a value of €430.

Travel Safety Advice

Visitors can get up-to-date travel safety information from the **Foreign and Commonwealth Office** in the UK, the **Department of State** in the US and the **Department of Foreign Affairs and Trade** in Australia.

Travel Insurance

EU citizens can avoid basic medical charges by carrying a valid **European Health Insurance Card** (EHIC), which must be obtained before travelling. (Note that dental care is not covered by EU health agreements.) Residents of other countries should purchase private medical cover before travel.

Health

No vaccinations are required for visiting Spain. Bring any medication that you require, and ideally a card in Spanish if you have a serious health issue, such as diabetes or epilepsy.

There are casualty departments (Urgencias) at the **Hospital General Gregorio Marañón** and **Hospital La Paz**. Other Spanish hospitals are listed in the Yellow Pages by area. For an English-speaking doctor or dentist contact the **Anglo-American Medical Unit**.

An illuminated green cross indicates a pharmacy (farmacia) and these are usually open from 10am to 2pm, and 5pm to 8pm Monday to Saturday. If closed, the address of the nearest alternative will be displayed in the window. Pharmacists will treat minor ailments as well as give medical advice – most speak a little English – but bring any prescription medicines with you as you may not be able to find the exact equivalent. Pharmacists can also provide information about nearby health centres and doctors.

Ask at your hotel or consult the Yellow Pages for the nearest dentist. **UDM Clínica Dental** covers 24-hour emergencies. Expect to pay at the time of treatment. The key emergency telephone number in Spain (for ambulance, police and fire brigade) is 112.

Personal Security

Madrid is a generally safe city, with little crime. Avoid travelling alone at night on empty streets or in metro carriages, and do not carry large amounts of cash. As in most cities, pickpockets target people in crowds, and at tourist sights. Keep your wallet out of sight and don't hang bags on the back of your chair in restaurants. Be careful of scams, such as strangers who tell you that you've dropped something. Don't purchase anything from a vendor who approaches you in the street.

Madrileños are not the most careful of drivers – jumping a red light is commonplace. Pedestrians do not have automatic right of way on crossings, and an orange flashing light is generally regarded as a "go" signal by drivers. Crossings are often on street corners, so keep an eye open for cars turning from the side roads.

Police stations, called comisarías, are listed in the Yellow Pages. You should report any crime, including theft and lost property, for insurance purposes. **The Foreign Tourist Assistance Service (SATE)** offers multilingual assistance from 9am to midnight, daily. If you lose your passport, inform your embassy or consulate, and the police. Foreign visitors can file a police report for most minor crimes from anywhere in Spain by calling this number: 902 102 112. English-speaking operators are available from 9am to 9pm, daily. For more information, visit www.policia.es.

Madrileños are generally very polite. Women travellers will not attract unwanted attention if they adopt the same precautions that they would take in any large city.

Disabled Travellers

The city's facilities for disabled travellers have improved considerably during the last decade, but there's still a long way to go. The tourist information office (see p139) publishes a useful leaflet called Accessible Tourism Guide to Madrid, available in Spanish and English as a downloadable PDF from its website. This recommends routes around the city suitable for disabled travellers, and provides an accessibility guide for all the important sights. City-run walking tours include options geared towards disabled travellers. The tourist information office can also provide a list of accessible hotels.

Most buses, train stations and some metro stations (marked on the metro map) are accessible.

Language

The official language in Madrid is Spanish. English is not widely spoken, except in hotels and some restaurants.

Driving Licence

All European and US driving licences are accepted in Spain. An International Driving Permit (IDP) for visitors from North America is recommended, but not mandatory.

DIRECTORY

CUSTOMS AND VISAS
Ⓦ agenciatributaria.es
Ⓦ exteriores.gob.es

TRAVEL SAFETY ADVICE
Australia
Department of Foreign Affairs and Trade
Ⓦ dfat.gov.au/smarttraveller.gov.au

United Kingdom
Foreign & Commonwealth Office
Ⓦ gov.uk/foreign-travel-advice

United States
US Department of State
Ⓦ travel.state.gov

EMERGENCY
Central Police Station/ Foreign Tourist Assistance Service (SATE)
C/Leganitos 19
Ⓒ 902 102 112

Fire, Ambulance and Police
Ⓒ 112

Municipal Police
Ⓒ 092

National Police
Ⓒ 091

LOST AN-D STOLEN CARDS
American Express
Ⓒ 902 37 56 37

MasterCard
Ⓒ 900 97 12 31

Visa
Ⓒ 900 99 12 16

HOSPITALS AND CLINICS
Anglo-American Medical Unit
Calle Conde de Aranda 1
Ⓒ 91 435 1823

Hospital General Gregorio Marañón
Calle Dr Esquerdo 46
Ⓒ 91 586 8000

Hospital La Paz
Paseo de la Castellana 261
Ⓒ 91 727 7000

Post Office
Paseo del Prado 1
Ⓒ 91 523 06 94
Ⓦ correos.es

UDM Clínica Dental
Calle Bretón de los Herreros 32
Ⓒ 91 441 4184

EMBASSIES AND CONSULATES
Canadian Embassy
Torre Espacio, Paseo de la Castellana 259D
Ⓒ 91 382 8400
Ⓦ canadainternational.gc.ca

Irish Embassy
Paseo de la Castellana 46-4
Ⓒ 91 436 40 93
Ⓦ dfa.ie/irish-embassy/Spain/

UK Embassy
Torre Espacio, Paseo de la Castellana 259
Ⓒ 917 14 63 00
Ⓦ gov.uk

USA Embassy
Serrano 75
Ⓒ 91 587 2200
Ⓦ madrid.usembassy.gov

DISABLED TRAVELLERS
Accessible Tourism
Ⓦ accessibletourism.org

Madrid Tourism
Ⓦ esmadrid.com/madrid-accesible

Currency and Banking

The official currency of Spain is the Euro. The Euro is subdivided into 100 *céntimos*. Euro bank-notes have the following denominations: 5, 10, 20, 50, 100, 200 and 500. Euro coins come in eight denominations: €1, €2, and 1, 2, 5, 10, 20 and 50 *céntimos*. Visitors from outside the eurozone should check the current exchange rates at the time of travel. It will usually be most cost-effective to buy currency in advance.

Casas de cambio are found throughout the city, especially around Puerta del Sol *(see p93)*. There are also 24-hour counters at Barajas airport *(see p134)*, the two mainline train stations, El Corte Inglés *(see p88)* and other central department stores and major hotels. Many banks also have a currency exchange desk. Banking hours are Monday to Friday, 8:30am to 2pm. Some branches also open from September to June only, on Saturdays from 9am to 1pm. During the San Isidro festival *(see p74)* all banks close at noon. ATMs abound in Madrid and offer the easiest way of getting hold of cash. Those accepting internationally recognized cards will give you a choice of several languages, including English. Most hotels and restaurants will take credit cards, but some smaller *pensions*, *tabernas* and *tapas* bars will accept only cash. Shops take cards but you may be asked to show some identification.

Communications

All Madrid phone numbers are prefixed with 91, followed by seven digits. Phone numbers must always be dialled in full, and include the city code. To phone Spain from overseas, dial the code 00 34. Public telephones take credit cards and phonecards, available from post offices, tobacconists and newspaper kiosks; only a few take coins. Local calls are inexpensive and all calls are cheaper between 8pm and 8am, and at weekends and on public holidays. A 3G broadband mobile will work in Spain, but check costs first with your provider. Spanish SIM cards or pay-as-you-go mobiles are widely available, and will avoid heavy roaming charges. Free Wi-Fi is available in a number of cafés, hotels and restaurants, as well as in international chains including Starbucks and McDonalds.

If you can read Spanish, most daily papers, such as *El País* and *El Mundo*, have a supplement on Madrid, including listings. *El País* also publishes an English-language supplement that rounds up Spanish news stories. Foreign newspapers and some magazines, such as *Time*, are available on the day of publication from kiosks. The kiosk at the western end of Puerta del Sol is open 24 hours.

Most big hotels subscribe to satellite and cable TV, and most TVs give you the option of watching in the original language. If you're staying in lower-priced accommodation you may have access only to the seven free Spanish channels – TVE1, TVE2, Antena 3, Telecinco, Cuatro, Telemadrid and La Sexta. There are six state radio stations, broadcasting in Spanish, plus several regional stations.

The main post office in Madrid is located at Paseo del Prado 1, and is open from 8:30am until 9:30pm Monday to Friday, and from 8:30am to 2pm on Saturdays. It offers a wide range of services, including express mail and parcel services, money transfers, and it also sells phone cards. There are several other branches around the city, which are usually open from 9:30am to 8:30pm Monday to Friday, and from 9:30am to 1pm on Saturdays. Postboxes are yellow, and are emblazoned with the "Correos" logo in dark blue. The service offered by the Spanish post office has improved enormously in recent years, and is on a par with that in most European countries in terms of delivery times and reliability. A letter or postcard from Spain to the UK will usually take 3 to 5 days, and from Spain to the US will take approximately 4 to 6 days.

Opening Hours

The month of August is extremely quiet as most *Madrileños* take their annual summer holidays at this time. While most tourist sights remain open to the public, you will find many bars and restaurants are closed.

In general, the shops in Madrid are open Monday to Saturday from 10am to 2pm, and 5pm to 8:30pm. Most downtown shops are also open on Sundays and holidays. Opening hours for department stores and larger shops and chains are Monday to Sunday 10am to 9pm. Museums have their own opening hours, although many are closed on Mondays.

Public holidays in Madrid are: New Year's Day (1 Jan), Epiphany (6 January), Feast of San José (19 March), Maundy Thursday, Good Friday, Labour Day (1 May), Feast of the Community of Madrid (2 May), Feast of San Isidro (15 May), Corpus Christi (4 June), Santiago Apostol Day (25 July), Ascension Day (15 August), Hispanic Day (12 Oct), All Saints' Day (1 Nov), Constitution Day (6 December), Immaculate Conception (8 December), and of course Christmas Day (25 December).

Time Difference

Madrid is on Central European Time, an hour ahead of GMT, and six hours ahead of Eastern Standard Time. Spanish summer time begins on the last Sunday in March and ends on the last Sunday in October.

Electrical Appliances

The local power supply is 220 volts AC. Wall sockets have two-pin plugs. You will require an adaptor for all electric appliances, such as hairdryers, shavers and laptops. If you are using an American appliance you'll need a transformer.

Tourist Information

The main city tourist office is in Plaza Mayor (see pp22–3), and is well-stocked with maps and brochures. The staff will help with accommodation but will not book it for you. The Comunidad de Madrid also has a tourist office, and can provide information on the Greater Madrid area, as well. Hi-tech tourist information mobile units situated at Palacio Real, Prado Museum and Caixa Forum are open during peak seasons and festivals. There are smaller tourist offices at Atocha and Chamartín railway stations, Plaza de Cibeles, Plaza del Callao and Plaza de Colón. Barajas airport (see p134) has two information centres in Terminals 2 and 4. Yellow information stands are also located in various terminals.

The official city website (www.esmadrid.com) has a number of free publications that can be downloaded from its website. These include maps, guides, ideas for walks, information on day trips and practical advice for disabled travellers, as well as the free monthly magazine which provides information about what's on in the city.

If you speak Spanish, interesting blogs include FotoMadrid (www.foto madrid.com), which is full of unusual photographs of the city, and Secretos de Madrid (www.secretos demadrid.es), which offers engaging insights into Madrid's hidden corners, as well as tips on unexpected things to see and do. The Madrid Cool blog (www.madridcool blog.com) has tips on where to eat and drink, as well as listings on the trendiest markets, and is also available in English.

When to Go

Madrid is idyllic in May and June, when the parks and gardens are blooming, and the city hosts its best traditional festival, the Fiesta de San Isidro (15 May). In August, the temperature soars, and many locals desert the city for the beach or mountains, but prices for accommodation drop considerably. September and October are equally enjoyable in terms of climate, but the city also has a special charm in winter, when the light is low (ideal for photography), the sky is a vivid blue, and there are no queues for the major attractions such as the Prado.

Weather

Madrid sits on a high plateau and has cold winters and hot, humid summers. The coldest months are January and February, with average temperatures ranging between 0° and 10° Celsius (32°–50° Fahrenheit). July and August can reach 35° Celsius (95° Fahrenheit).

Websites

Numerous websites cover Madrid, including the official Tourist Office site (www.esmadrid.com). Another useful resource is www.madrid.es, the city council's website. The Madrid region (Comunidad de Madrid) has its own website (http://turismomadrid.es), with extensive coverage of the whole region. Useful apps include City Maps and Walks and GPS My City, which provide detailed self-guided walks. These are available offline as well. Another app is the Madrid EMT | Metro | Renfe app (available from iTunes), which provides travel information for public transport, including a route planner. Other apps include TripAdvisor, for reviews of attractions, hotels and restaurants; Urban Step, for bus times; and Google Translate or iTranslate, for translations.

Shopping

Madrid is a world-class shopping destination, offering everything from vintage and cutting-edge fashion to gourmet treats. You'll find all the popular Spanish chains, from Zara (see p97) to Camper, along the Gran Vía, while the Chueca and Malasaña districts offer one-off boutiques and vintage shopping (see pp122-3).

Top international and home-grown fashion labels are found in upmarket Salamanca (see pp84–91). Foodies shouldn't miss Madrid's markets, where the stalls are piled high with every imaginable type of produce.

Bargain-hunters should note that winter sales start after the Three Kings celebration on 6 January, and summer sales begin on 1 July.

VAT (IVA) is currently 21 per cent on most goods. Non-EU residents can apply for tax refunds on purchases that cost over €99 when they are bought at participating stores. You will be given a form to be stamped at airport customs, and can claim your refund at a *casa de cambio* or bank.

Dining

Madrileños love to eat, and the city's dining scene offers something for everyone, from humble *tapas* bars to Michelin-starred establishments featuring the creations of world-famous chefs. The hearty local cuisine, as you might expect from an inland region, features plenty of stews and roast meats, but Madrid is also, rather surprisingly for a city so far from the coast, famed for its seafood, flown in freshly each morning from the ports of northern Spain. You can take a culinary tour of all Spain in Madrid, where there are restaurants offering the cuisines from every part of the country. Restaurants serving good international food are on the increase, offering everything from borscht

to pad thai. Vegetarian and vegan eateries, while still rare, can now be found dotted across the city.

Restaurants usually open from 1:30 or 2pm to 3:30 or 4pm for lunch, and from 8:30 or 9pm to 11pm or midnight for dinner. If you prefer to eat earlier, fill up at one of the many tapas restaurants which are usually open from 7pm or even earlier. Restaurants are often closed on Sunday evenings and on Mondays.

Many restaurants, including some of the city's best, offer a great value *menú del día* (set lunch) on weekdays. This is a good way to try some top-notch cuisine without breaking your budget. Some restaurants will also offer a *menú infantil* (children's menu) but they are not very common. *Tapas* are ideal for kids, providing small portions of plenty of different foods, and cafés are regularly open all day for light fare. If you need a highchair, rarely available at restaurants, bring your own or phone ahead.

Smoking

Smoking is prohibited in hotels, bars, restaurants, clubs and cafés across Spain, although a few have set up designated outdoor smoking areas. Smoking is also banned in all public buildings, such as hospitals, and on public transport. However, smoking is much more commonplace than in many other countries, such as the UK or the USA, and you will find, for example, that café and bar terraces are full of smokers, and that smoking is perfectly common at bus stops and in other public places.

Tours

The hop-on, hop-off **Madrid City Tour** service operates from 10am to 6pm between November and February, and from 9am to 10pm from March to October. There are two routes: both cover the Paseo del Prado, then the blue route heads west around the Royal Palace, and the green route goes north to Salamanca and the Bernabéu Stadium. Tickets are available for one or two days (€21/€25 for adults, or €10/€13 for children under 7).

The tourist office *(see p139)* organizes a wide range of walking tours, including some geared towards disabled travellers. Themes include art and literary tours, haunted Madrid, and even crime and mystery tours. Tickets can be purchased at the tourist office, through **Entradas**, at **Bankia** ATM terminals or by calling Bankia direct.

Bravo Bike runs city tours with a choice of standard or electric bikes (some streets in the old centre are very steep). It also offers tours of towns outside Madrid, including bike tours of El Escorial, Aranjuez and Toledo. You could also take a tour of Madrid on a **Segway:** tours of the essential sights, restaurant tours and flamenco tours are just some of the options available. Tours include a useful initial training session.

Another fun alternative is to scoot around the city in a vintage **Seat 600**. There is a choice of three routes, and prices can include lunch or a pit stop for *chocolate con churros* (hot chocolate with fried dough strips), if required.

Where to Stay

Madrid used to be cursed with a lack of characterful accommodation, but now it offers a wealth of options in all price categories. Whether you're looking for deluxe hotel with all the trimmings or a cosy guesthouse, you'll find something to suit your taste and budget.

Accommodation fills up quickly during holidays and events such as big trade fairs, so be advised to book well in advance. Room prices usually decrease in August, particularly at the chain hotels, which largely cater for business clients.

Accommodation in Spain falls into the following categories: hotels, rated with between one and five stars; hostals, which are simple guesthouses that often resemble hotels, and shouldn't be confused with youth hostels; B&Bs; holiday apartments; youth hostels, which generally offer dormitory or shared accommodation; and student residences, which provide inexpensive accommodation during the summer break. The nearest campsite to the city, **Camping Osuna** provides basic facilities near the airport and close to the Metro.

The Madrid tourist office provides a comprehensive online database of a variety of accommodation options in all categories, but it does not provide a booking service. Book directly with your accommodation choice, or via one of the online booking portals.

Light sleepers should pack earplugs, as street noise lasts well into the night, particularly at weekends. Alternatively, ask for a quieter, interior room (many hotels have a peaceful internal courtyard), or one on a less busy side street.

Places to Stay

PRICE CATEGORIES
For a standard, double room per night (with breakfast if included), taxes and extra charges.
€ under €120   €€ 120–240   €€€ over €240

Luxury Hotels

Miguel Angel
MAP F1 ■ Miguel Angel 29–31 ■ 91 442 0022 ■ www.hotelmiguelangel.com ■ €

From the outside, this modern hotel overlooking Paseo de la Castellana, conforms with the high-rise architecture typical of the business district, but the interior, refurbished with antiques, is a surprise. Facilities include a sun terrace, an indoor pool, sauna, gym and disco. The M29 restaurant serves innovative Mediterranean cuisine.

Villa Real
MAP E4 ■ Plaza de las Cortes 10 ■ 91 420 3767 ■ www.hotelvillareal.com ■ Dis. access ■ €

The elegant Villa Real opened in 1989. The antique decor extends to the luxury suites, while the foyer is decorated with Roman mosaics. Facilities include a fitness suite, conference centre and a gourmet restaurant.

Gran Meliá Fénix
MAP G2 ■ Calle Hermosilla 2 ■ 91 431 6700 ■ www.melia.com ■ Dis. access ■ €€

This gorgeous hotel is located near Plaza Colón. It is handy for the sights and the Salamanca shopping district.

The Principal
MAP R3 ■ Calle Marqués de Valdeiglesias 1 ■ 91 521 8743 ■ www.theprincipal madridhotel.com ■ Dis. access ■ €€

This occupies a splendid century-old building, and features elegant, contemporary rooms, a fabulous rooftop terrace and a restaurant with Michelin-starred chef Ramón Freixa at the helm.

Santo Mauro
MAP F1 ■ Calle Zurbano 36 ■ 91 319 6900 ■ www.marriott.com ■ €€

Small, elegant hotel enjoying a secluded leafy location only a five-minute walk from the Paseo de la Castellana. The former palace was refurbished in the 1990s in a mixture of classical and modern styles. The ballrooms now serve as conference rooms while the library is a gourmet restaurant with terrace. Indoor swimming pool.

Wellington
MAP G3 ■ Calle Velázquez 8 ■ 91 575 4400 ■ www.hotelwellington.com ■ €€

During the San Isidro festival in May, this hotel is the first choice for Spain's top bullfighters. Its Michelin-starred restaurant, Kabuki, serves Japanese–Spanish fusion cuisine. The swimming pool is a bonus.

Westin Palace
MAP E4 ■ Plaza de las Cortes 7 ■ 91 360 8000 ■ www.westinpalace madrid.com ■ Dis. access ■ €€

This hotel opened in 1913 and has been wowing guests ever since with its opulence. The palatial facilities include 18 banqueting and conference rooms, a business centre, fitness suite and a gourmet restaurant.

Hotel Hospes
MAP G3 ■ Pl de la Independencia 3 ■ 91 432 2911 ■ www.hotelhospesmadrid.com ■ Dis. access ■ €€€

Overlooking the Retiro Gardens, this chic boutique hotel is ideally located for shopping in Salamanca or for visiting the Prado. A sumptuous mansion-turned-hotel, its chic guest rooms are complemented by a spa and an elegant restaurant.

Ritz
MAP F4 ■ Plaza de la Lealtad 5 ■ 91 701 6767 ■ www.ritz.es ■ Dis. access ■ €€€

Madrid's oldest luxury hotel remains true to the traditional values of refined comfort and impeccable service. The *belle époque* decor and furnishings are seen to best effect in the restaurant, which overlooks a flower-filled garden. Facilities include a gym and a sauna (see p80).

Villa Magna
MAP G2 ■ Paseo de la Castellana 22 ■ 91 587 1234 ■ www.villamagna.es ■ Dis. access ■ €€€

What attracts celebrities

to this hotel is the service and attention to detail. The restaurant is a byword for fine dining, and the 150 rooms are spacious and elegant.

Historic Hotels

Catalonia Plaza Mayor

MAP N5 ▪ Calle de Atocha 36 ▪ 91 369 4409 ▪ www.hoteles-catalonia.com ▪ €

The Catalonia Plaza Mayor could not be more central. This great value hotel is set in a 19th- century building just a few steps from the famous Plaza Mayor. The interiors are resolutely modern, but the twirling wrought-iron balconies have been preserved. Extra benefits include a tranquil courtyard and fitness centre.

Hostal Greco

MAP R2 ▪ Calle Infantas 3, 2nd floor ▪ 91 522 4632 ▪ www.hostalgreco.com ▪ Dis. access ▪ €

This was once a brothel catering for a wealthy clientele that included members of Spain's aristocracy. Signs of its history include frescoes depicting women striking seductive poses. The location near the Gran Vía is excellent.

Posada del Peine

MAP M4 ▪ Calle Postas 17 ▪ 91 523 8151 ▪ www.hpetitpalaceposadadelpeine.com ▪ Dis. access ▪ €

This charming hotel, founded in 1610, is the oldest in Spain and is conveniently located on a pedestrian street in the heart of Old Madrid, close to the Plaza Mayor. Some

rooms are small, but the decor is modern and there are computers and Wi-Fi in each room. Small pets are allowed.

AC Palacio del Retiro

MAP G4 ▪ Calle de Alfonso XII 14 ▪ 91 523 7460 ▪ €€

Set in a handsome mansion dating back to 1907, this hotel boasts views of the Retiro Gardens. The charming rooms pair period details such as ceiling mouldings and original hardwood floors with 21st-century extras including iPod docks and plasma TVs. A restaurant and spa are among the other amenities.

Adler

MAP G2 ▪ Calle Velázquez 33 ▪ 91 4263 220 ▪ www.adlerhotelmadrid.com ▪ Dis. access ▪ €€

Another of the plush boutique hotels in Madrid's elegant Salamanca district, this has stylish interior decor by Pascua Ortega, which evokes the mansion's 19th-century origins, and conserves its elegant galleries and balconies. Works by Miró, Chillida and Tàpies adorn the walls.

Innside Madrid Suecia

MAP R3 ▪ Calle Marqués de Casa Riera 4 ▪ 91 200 0570 ▪ €€

The original Hotel Suecia was opened in the 1950s by the Swedish royal family, and famous former guests have included Ernest Hemingway and Che Guevara. After years of neglect, it was bought and remodelled into a

stylish, contemporary hotel in 2014, and now offers chic guest rooms and a rooftop terrace with plunge pool.

Las Letras Gran Vía

MAP Q3 ▪ Gran Vía 11 ▪ 91 523 7980 ▪ www.hoteldelasletras.com ▪ Dis. access ▪ €€

This graceful hotel occupies a Neo-Classical building which preserves its original sweeping staircase and elaborate mouldings. The walls of the modern rooms are inscribed with quotes by celebrated writers, and the best rooms have private terraces with jacuzzis. Don't miss the views from the chic rooftop terrace.

NH Palacio de Tepa

MAP R5 ▪ Calle de San Sebastián 2 ▪ 91 389 6490 ▪ Dis. access ▪ €€

In Madrid's famous Barrio de las Letras, this 19th-century townhouse has been transformed into a contemporary boutique hotel with a modern interior. The beamed ceilings, elaborate columns and floor-to-ceiling windows in some rooms recall its original glory days.

Splendom Suites

MAP Q5 ▪ Calle San Onofres 5 ▪ 91 531 9068 ▪ www.splendomsuitesmadrid.com ▪ €€

This four-star hotel is located just a two-minute walk away from the Gran Vía and offers luxury and comfort at a good price. Deluxe suites and studios come with their own kitchen areas. There are parking spaces available in the building.

Orfila

MAP F2 ■ Orfila 6 ■ 91 702 7770 ■ www.hotel orfila.com ■ €€€

Built in 1886 as a palatial townhouse, the Orfila is located in a leafy part of town near Colón. The 20 rooms and 12 suites are tastefully decorated in soft pinks and yellows to create a relaxed ambience. A small restaurant overlooks a secluded garden.

Design Hotels

Abalú

MAP M1 ■ Calle Pez 19 ■ 91 531 4744 ■ www. hotelabalu.com ■ €

Each of the rooms and apartments here has been individually designed in a colourful, eclectic style. Some rooms also boast a private balcony. The stylish suites have a separate lounge with a home cinema, and bathrooms with a Jacuzzi or Thai stone bath.

Be Live City Center Santo Domingo

MAP L2 ■ Calle San Bernardo 1 ■ 91 547 9800 ■ www.hotelssantodomin go.es ■ Dis. access ■ €

This modernized hotel, convenient for the Palacio Real and the Gran Vía, is furnished with strategically placed statues and old paintings to give it a touch of elegance. Though small, the rooms are comfortable – book one on the fifth floor where there are tiny balconies with lovely views over the rooftops of the city.

Hostal Gala

MAP L3 ■ Costanilla de los Ángeles 15, 2a ■ 91 541 9692 ■ www. hostalgala.com ■ €

If you're looking for style on a budget, this guesthouse is a great choice. The air-conditioned rooms and apartments are compact, but feature chic, modern decor, and the friendly staff go out of their way to make guests feel at home.

Hotel Life

MAP M1 ■ Calle Pizarro 16 ■ 91 531 4744 ■ www. hotellifemadrid.es ■ €

The bright, modern rooms at this good value hotel feature original upcycled furnishings and art, and a mixture of contemporary and vintage decor. Convenient extras include free Wi-Fi and laptop hire, and the lively bars and cafés of the Malasaña district on the doorstep.

Hotel Meninas

MAP L3 ■ Calle Campomanes 7 ■ 91 541 2805 ■ www.hotel meninas.es ■ €

This small boutique hotel near the Opera House features simple but inviting rooms, elegantly decorated and with floor-to-ceiling windows which open out onto a small balcony. Soothing colours are brought up-to-date with splashes of bright colour.

Posada del Dragón

MAP L6 ■ Cava Baja 14 ■ 91 119 1424 ■ www. posadadeldragon.com ■ €

Sections of medieval wall and an attractive wooden staircase are preserved in this 16th-century inn, but the guest rooms are entirely contemporary with their bold colours and modern lights and furnishings.

The trendy restaurant – one of many that line the Cava Baja – serves tasty local cuisine. It's a lively area so ask for a room at the back if you prefer a quiet night.

Room-Mate Alicia

MAP Q5 ■ Calle del Prado 2 ■ 91 389 6095 ■ www. room-matehotels.com ■ €

This modern hotel, conveniently located in the Plaza de Santa Ana, is an ideal choice for those keen to enjoy Madrid's nightlife. The colourful rooms have large windows that look out over this vibrant square.

ME Madrid

MAP P5 ■ Plaza de Sta Ana 14 ■ 91 701 6000 ■ www.melia.com ■ Dis. access ■ €€

Refurbishments have converted this beautiful early 1900s building into a modern hotel with great facilities and a trendy, penthouse bar. The hotel is a much-loved landmark, conveniently located close to Puerta del Sol and the city's museums.

Only You Hotel

MAP E3 ■ Calle Barquillo 21 ■ 91 005 2222 ■ www. onlyyouhotels.com ■ €€

Catalan designer Lázaro Rosa-Violán is responsible for the striking decor at this trendy hotel, which occupies a 19th-century mansion in the Chueca neighbourhood. Many rooms have original wood beamed ceilings, which are paired with contemporary wallpaper and furnishings. Visitors can relax in the lounge bar, set in a former bookshop.

Hotel Único
MAP G2 ▪ Calle Claudio Coello 67 ▪ 91 781 0173 ▪ www.unicohotel madrid.com ▪ €€€

A firm favourite with the fashion crowd, this stylish boutique hotel occupies a beautifully remodelled 19th-century mansion in upmarket Salamanca. As well as a Michelin-starred restaurant and a charming courtyard garden, it boasts a range of extra services such as personal shoppers.

Business Hotels

Catalonia Gran Vía
MAP R3 ▪ Gran Vía 9 ▪ 91 531 2222 ▪ www.hoteles-catalonia.es ▪ €

Conveniently situated on the stock exchange, this comfortable hotel is also handy for sightseeing. The modern rooms offer satellite TV, and facilities include a Catalan restaurant, a gym and sauna.

Exe Moncloa
MAP B2 ▪ Calle Arcipreste Hita 10 ▪ 91 745 9299 ▪ www.hotelexemoncloa.com ▪ Dis. access ▪ €

Located in front of the Intercambiador de Moncloa Metro and bus hub, this modern hotel offers a comfortable stay, with good facilities for business travellers. It also has a swimming pool.

Hotel H10 Orense
Calle de Pedro Teixeira 5 ▪ 91 597 1568 ▪ www.h10hotels.com ▪ €

This 4-star hotel is in an excellent location within Madrid's business district. Facilities include three meeting rooms, a private dining room and Wi-Fi.

Ilunion Suites
Calle López de Hoyos 143 ▪ Metro Alfonso XIII ▪ 91 744 5000 ▪ www.ilunion suitesmadrid.com ▪ Dis. access ▪ €

North of the centre, this hotel has 120 suites, all equipped with satellite TV. Facilities include a restaurant offering international cuisine.

Meliá Barajas
Avenida de Logroño 305 ▪ 91 747 7700 ▪ www.melia.com ▪ Dis. access ▪ €

On the approach road to Barajas airport, this 229-room modern hotel is convenient for the IFEMA Exhibition Centre. Rooms are comfortable and the facilities include a garden, outdoor pool, restaurants, gym and meeting rooms.

NH Madrid Ribera de Manzanares
MAP OFF MAP AT B6 ▪ Paseo Virgen del Puerto 57 ▪ 91 364 3248 ▪ www.nh-hotels.com ▪ €

Overlooking the Manzanares River, this modern hotel offers great value accommodation, plus 12 meeting rooms, a planning service for conferences and other events, and convenient extras such as private parking, a gym, and a restaurant and bar. The junior suites all enjoy wonderful views over the old town.

La Posada del Chaflán
Avenida de Pío XII 34 ▪ 91 345 0450 ▪ www.lapos adadeelchaflan.com ▪ €

The main advantage of this small, modern hotel is the location – 15 minutes' drive from the airport, IFEMA Exhibition Centre, Palace of Congresses and the city. The restaurant serves Andalusian cuisine and has a small terrace.

AC-Aitana
MAP F3 ▪ Paseo de la Castellana 152 ▪ 91 458 4970 ▪ www.marriott.com ▪ Dis. access ▪ €€

The facilities at this functional, fully renovated 4-star business hotel include on-site parking, a restaurant and bar, reading room, fitness centre and two small conference rooms. All rooms are equipped with satellite TV, two phones and Wi-Fi.

InterContinental Hotel
MAP G1 ▪ Paseo de la Castellana 49 ▪ 91 700 7300 ▪ www.ihg.com ▪ €€

A wide choice of meeting and conference rooms, a dedicated concierge team and excellent facilities including a 24-hour business centre have made this luxury hotel in Madrid's main financial district a winner with business travellers. Unwind in the 24-hour fitness centre or indulge in some spa pampering.

Radisson Blu Prado Hotel Madrid
MAP F5 ▪ Calle Moratín 52 ▪ 91 524 2626 ▪ www.radissonblu.com ▪ €€

Offering large rooms with plenty of space in which to work, this sleekly designed hotel offers all the usual amenities for the business traveller, including meeting rooms and a business centre. Other amenities include a luxurious spa, a whisky bar and a superb location right opposite the Prado.

Budget Accommodation

Alojamiento Carrera
MAP Q4 ▪ Carrera de San Jerónimo 30, 3rd floor ▪ 91 429 6808 ▪ www.alojamientocarrera.com ▪ €
An easy-going, friendly place with a great location near Sol and the nightlife of Santa Ana. The rooms are generously sized, but those overlooking the street can be noisy.

Artrip
MAP E6 ▪ Calle Valencia 11 ▪ 91 539 3282 ▪ www.artriphotel.com ▪ €
Set in a turn-of-the-20th-century townhouse, the pretty guest rooms at this charming small hotel feature subtle, white-on-white decor. Local artists show their work throughout the hotel in changing exhibitions, and the delightful staff are happy to provide tips on what to see and do nearby.

Hostal Gonzalo
MAP F5 ▪ Calle Cervantes 34, 3rd floor ▪ 91 429 2714 ▪ www.hostalgonzalo.com ▪ €
A pleasant hostel in a historic part of Madrid, close to the museums of the Paseo del Prado. Some of the rooms have balconies with rooftop views of the city and are surprisingly quiet, bearing in mind that this area is known for its nightlife.

Hostal La Prensa
MAP M2 ▪ Gran Vía 46, 8º ▪ 91 531 9307 ▪ www.hostallaprensa.com. €
With views of the Gran Vía, this delightful guesthouse has high-ceilinged, cosy rooms decorated in colourful prints and all with air conditioning and private bathrooms. It's set in one of Madrid's oldest skyscrapers, built in the 1920s.

Hostal Persal
MAP P5 ▪ Plaza del Angel 12 ▪ 91 369 4643 ▪ www.hostalpersal.com ▪ €
Located overlooking a peaceful square, and yet surrounded by shops, bars and monuments, this hostel is excellent value. The comfortable rooms all have satellite TV and some overlook the courtyard. It also has its own coffee shop, which is a good place to get to know fellow guests and to trade information.

Hotel Francisco I
MAP D4 ▪ Calle Arenal 15 ▪ 91 548 0204 ▪ www.hotelfrancisco.com ▪ €
This cosy little hotel is situated in the very heart of Madrid and is only a stone's throw from key city sights such as Puerta del Sol, Plaza Mayor and the Palacio Real. All 65 rooms have been stylishly refurbished, and you'll find all the standard hotel amenities, with the bonus of a games room.

Lapepa Chic B&B
MAP F4 ▪ Plaza de las Cortes 4 ▪ 64 847 4742 ▪ www.lapepa-bnb.com ▪ €
Just a stone's throw from Madrid's great trio of big museums, this warm and friendly B&B offers stylish rooms decorated in bright colours, and a cosy lounge with a kitchen corner where guests can gather for breakfast. Service is excellent and iPod docks are available.

Mora
MAP F5 ▪ Paseo del Prado 32 ▪ 91 420 1569 ▪ www.hotelmora.com ▪ €
Art lovers on a budget should look no further than this modest-sized hotel, just across the road from the Prado. Some rooms have views of the famous avenue. Room safes and satellite TV are other pluses. It's very popular, so book ahead.

TOC Hostel
MAP N4 ▪ Plaza Celenque 3-5 ▪ 91 532 1304 ▪ www.tochostels.com ▪ €
One of the new breed of designer hostels, this offers a choice of funkily decorated private guest rooms or dorms. Get to know your fellow travellers in the bar, or over a game of pool. Whip up some dinner in the well-equipped kitchen.

Hotels with a Difference

Hotel Emperador
MAP P2 ▪ Gran Vía 53 ▪ 91 547 2800 ▪ www.emperadorhotel.com ▪ Dis. access ▪ €
This hotel is in a great location overlooking Plaza de España. Its luxurious rooms (suites have their own Jacuzzis and hydro-massage showers) make it the first choice for many celebrities. There's also a rooftop swimming pool.

NH Abascal
MAP G2 ▪ Calle José Abascal 47 ▪ 91 441 0015 ▪ www.nh-hotels.com ▪ Dis. access ▪ €
This hotel was once the Lebanese embassy. The decor is suitably aristocratic, with lavish use of marble and wrought iron.

The rooms are tastefully furnished and are all equipped with cable TV. Facilities include a sauna, 24-hour gym and a terrace restaurant.

Ópera

MAP L3 ▪ Cuesta de S Domingo 2 ▪ 91 541 2800 ▪ www.hotelopera.com ▪ €

As its name suggests, this comfortable 4-star hotel is close to the Opera House. All rooms have satellite TV and some have balconies. The English-speaking staff are helpful, and every evening at 9:30pm the waiters in the Café de la Ópera restaurant serenade guests with arias.

Petit Palace Arenal

MAP M4 ▪ Calle Arenal 16 ▪ 91 564 4355 ▪ www. hotelpetitpalacearenal. com ▪ €

Madrid is slowly becoming more bike-friendly, and at this central hotel you can borrow bikes for free. The hotel also provides other handy freebies for the pocket-conscious traveller, such as the free use of an iPad. Families will appreciate the multi-bed rooms that sleep up to six, and the use of buggies and cots.

Room Mate Óscar

MAP Q2 ▪ Plaza de Pedro Zerolo 12 ▪ 91 701 1173 ▪ oscar.room-matehotels.com ▪ €

Part of the popular Room Mate chain, this hotel has ultra-stylish, modern rooms decorated in vibrant colours, but the highlight is undoubtedly the rooftop sun deck and swimming pool. There's a poolside bar,

and DJ sessions make it particularly popular on sultry summer nights.

Silken Puerta América

Avenida de América 41 ▪ 91 744 5400 ▪ www. hoteles-silken.com ▪ €

The brainchild of French architect Jean Nouvel, this modern hotel is located on one of the main arteries into the centre of Madrid. Each of its 12 floors has been designed by a well-known architect or designer, including Norman Foster, Arata Isozaki, Zaha Hadid and Javier Mariscal. The hotel also has a good restaurant.

Eurostars Madrid Tower

Paseo de la Castellana 259 B ▪ 91 334 2700 ▪ www.eurostars madridtower.com ▪ €€

This hotel is set in the PwC Tower, which forms part of the Cuatro Torres business district, and is one of the tallest buildings in Madrid. Enjoy breath-taking panoramic views from the pool in the spa and health club, or from the gastronomic Volvoreta restaurant on the 30th floor.

Hotel Atlántico

MAP N2 ▪ Gran Vía 38 ▪ 91 522 6480 ▪ www. hotelatlantico.es ▪ €€

This hotel is a favourite with guests, who keep coming back thanks to its comfortable, classically decorated rooms, its charming service and its fantastically central location. But the icing on the cake is without doubt the gorgeous rooftop terrace, where

you can enjoy a drink and watch the sun set over the ancient rooftops of the historic city centre.

NH Collection Madrid Eurobuilding

Calle Padre Damián 23 ▪ 91 353 7300 ▪ www.nh-hotels.es ▪ Dis. access ▪ €€

In Madrid's main business district, this glossy hotel has a huge LED-domed screen in the lobby, and its Living Lab guest rooms come with high-tech features such as ultra HD TVs and intelligent lighting. Rooms on the highest floors have breathtaking views, and dining options include DiverXO, Madrid's only restaurant with three Michelin stars.

Urso Hotel & Spa

MAP E2 ▪ Calle Mejía Lequerica 8 ▪ 91 444 4458 ▪ hotelurso.com ▪ €€

Spacious, fashionably decorated guest rooms, wonderful staff and a great full-service spa by Natura Bissé, complete with a small heated pool, make this ideal for a luxurious urban break. The best rooms have French doors leading out onto private terraces.

VP El Jardín de Recoletos

MAP G3 ▪ Calle Gil de Santivanes 6 ▪ 91 781 16 40 ▪ www.recoletos-hotel.com ▪ €€

This hotel has a beautiful garden terrace, an oasis of green in the heart of the city. Comfortably furnished rooms are light and airy, and you can dine on traditional Mediterranean cuisine amid the magnolias and palm trees in the hotel's romantic restaurant.

General Index

Acknowledgments

The Authors

Christopher & Melanie Rice have travelled throughout Europe writing guides to destinations from the Algarve to the Turkish coast. They have been visiting Madrid for more than 20 years and have now decided to make it their home.

Additional contributor
Mary-Ann Gallagher

Publishing Director Georgina Dee

Publisher Vivien Antwi

Design Director Phil Ormerod

Editorial Michelle Crane, Alice Fewery, Rachel Fox, Fay Franklin, Freddie Marriage, Fíodhna Ní Ghríofa, Ellen Root, Sally Schafer

Design Richard Czapnik, Sunita Gahir, Rahul Kumar

Cartography Suresh Kumar, Casper Morris, Reetu Pandey

Picture Research Phoebe Lowndes, Susie Peachey, Ellen Root, Oran Tarjan

DTP Jason Little, George Nimmo

Production Linda Dare

Factchecker Lynnette McCurdy Bastida

Proofreader Laura Walker

Indexer Hilary Bird

Illustrator Chris Orr & Associates

Commissioned Photography Barnabas Kindersley, Lisa Linder, Rough Guides/Ian Aitken, Rough Guides/Tim Draper, Rough Guides/Lydia Evans, Kim Sayer, Clive Streeter; John Whittaker, Peter Wilson.

First edition created by Sargasso Media Ltd, London

Picture Credits

The publisher would like to thank the following for their kind permission to reproduce their photographs:
Key: a-above; b-below/bottom; c-centre; f-far; l-left; r-right; t-top

Al Natural: Andres Arranz Pinto 99tl.

Alamy Images: age fotostock 23cr, 88tl, 93cr, 128tl, /Guillermo Navarro 61br, /José Ramiro 63clb; Peter Barritt 20tl; blickwinkel 26br; Danita Delimont 25tr; Emma Durnford 115cr; epa european pressphoto agency b.v. 74cl; Factofoto 53br, 94c; Kevin Foy 65tl; Maria Galan 112clb; Kevin George 52tl; Hemis 14br; Heritage Image Partnership Ltd 18br; Phil Hill 91cr; Peter Horree 38cl, 90bl, 108tr; INTERFOTO/Monasterio de Las Descalzas Reales,Madrid *La Dolorosa*, by Pedro de Mena 100tl, /Museo del Prado, Madrid *The Adoration of the Shepherds* (1612) by El Greco 16clb; Stefano Politi Markovina 51tr; Masterpics/Prado Museum *Carlos III* (1761) by Anton Rafael Mengs 15tl, /Prado Museum *Self Portrait* (1498) by Albrecht Durer 21tl, /Prado Museum *Autodafe on Plaza Mayor with Charles II* (1680) by Francisco Rizi 46t; Melba Photo Agency 53tl; North Wind Picture Archives 46cb; Alberto Paredes 59bc; PjrTravel 26cl; Sergio Pitamitz 25br; Prisma Archivo 84cb, *Battle of Turin, 1706* by Joseph Parrocel 15b; RosalreneBetancourt 6 88crb; SAGAPHOTO.COM/Patrick Forget 118tl; Alex Segre 86cr; Sueddeutsche Zeitung Photo/Giribas Jose 67cra; World History Archive 35tl; Zoonar GmbH 62c, 80b, 95bl.

Jamones Julián Becerro: 113br.

El Bocaito: 69cla, 125tr.

Bodega Santa Cecilia: Goyo Conde 73cl.

La Bola: Picasa 105tr.

Bridgeman Images: De Agostini Picture Library 14cl; Museo Lazaro Galdiano, Madrid *The Adoration of the Magi* (1567-70) by El Greco(Domenico Theotocopuli) 85br; Prado, Madrid *Las Meninas or The Family of Philip IV* (c.1656) by Diego Rodriguez de Silva y Velazquez 16br.

Capas Seseña: 72cl.

Casa Alberto: 117cl.

Casa Museo Sorolla: *Walk by the Sea* (1909) by Joaquin Sorolla 49cr; *The Horse's Bath* (1909) by Joaquin Sorolla 87bl.

Casa Patas: 115tc.

Corbis: Arcaid/Richard Bryant 13tl; Eye Ubiquitous/Bennett Dean 112tr; The Gallery Collection 18tl; Hemis/René Mattes 41tl; Leemage/Prado Museum *The Spinners or The Fable of Arachne* (c.1657) by Diego Velazquez 17tl.

Delic: Gonzalo Mayoral Corral 116cla.

Dreamstime.com: Achilles 11cr; Alezia 11tl; Anibaltrejo 92tl; Bpperry 10cr, 109bl; Byvalet 57bl; Dennis Dolkens 6tl, 60t; Dinozzaver 107tr; Drfail 103bl; Epalaciosan 95tl; Gil7416 56t; Gilles Gaonach 2tl, 8-9; Greg0y108 54-5; Hect 51cl;Hemero-skopion 75tl; Icononiac 62t; Jackf 127tl; Javierespuny 7cr; Justinmetz 37cr; Karsol 129bc; Lawmoment 74tr; Lucavanzolini 61cla; Lucvar 68cla; Macsim 40-1; Andres Garcia Martin 4b; Miff32 4crb; Mtrommer 127br; Nikolais 80tr; Nito100 26-7; Oscar273 101t; Outsiderzone 37tl, 126tl; Pabkov 41cr, 57cr; Paha_l 36br; Sedmak 78tl, 102tr; Siempreverde22 12-13, 23tl; Slowcentury 26bl, 106tl; Tomas1111 3tl, 76-7; Tonnywu76 129tl; Tupungato 63tr, 97cl; David Pereiras Villagrá 96br; Vwalakte 7tr.

Festival de Otoño a Primavera: Herve All 75cl.

Getty Images: DEA/A. Dagli Orti 47tr; DeAgostini 43b; Pablo Blazquez Dominguez 74bl; Hulton Archive 43tl, /Culture Club 47cl; UIG/MyLoupe 90tc.

La Kitchen: 124clb.

La Manduca de Azagra: Estudio 52 124tc.

La Parra: 130crb.

La Tienda de las Hamacas: 114br.

La Violeta: 113tc. **Loewe :** 89bl.

Madrid Destino: Sofía Menendez 79t.

Manuel Gonzalez Contreras: 72tr.

Meliá Hotels: Thierry Delsart 67b, 116br.

Meson Cuevas Del Vino: 131br.

© Museo Thyssen-Bornemisza, Madrid: *Young Knight in a Landscape* (1510) by Vittore Carpaccio 28bl; *Swaying Dancer* (1877-9) by Edgar Degas 30bc; *Christ and Woman of Samaria at the Well* (1310-1) by Duccio di Buoninsegna 28-9; *The Annunciation* (c.1567-1577) by El Greco 29crb; *Portrait of Henry VIII of England* (1537) by Hans Holbein The Younger 29tc; *Hotel Room* (1931) by Edward Hopper 31br; *Still Life with Instruments* (1915) by Liubov Popova 31tl; *Woman with a Parasol in a Garden* (c.1873) by Pierre-Auguste Renoir 30tl.

Museo Arqueologico Nacional: Santiago Relanzón 38bc, 38-9, 39tl, 39ca, 39cb, 39b.

Museo Cerralbo: Latova José Fernández-Luna 48t.

Museo Chicote: Emilia Brandao 66t, emiliabrandaophoto 98bl.

Museo del Romanticismo: Pablo Linés Viñuales 119tr.

Museo Nacional Centro de Arte Reina Sofía: Joaquin Cortes/ Roman Lores 11tc, 79bl; *Mujer sentada I (Seated Woman)* (ca. 1935) sculpture by Julio Gonzalez 34bl; *Retrato II (1938)* by Joan Miro © Successió Miró/ADAGP, Paris and DACS London 2016 33cr; *Guernica* (1937) by Pablo Picasso © Succession Picasso/DACS, London 2016 35b; *Accidente Also known as Self-portrait* (1936) by Alfonso Ponce de León 33tr; *Le tertulia del Cafe de Pombo* (1920) by Jose Gutierrez Solana © DACS 2016 32bl.

NH Hoteles/Estado Puro: Gonzalo Arche 71clb.

Palacio de Cibeles: 83c.

Parque de Atracciones: 58bl.

Patrimonio Nacional: 24cr.

Reserva y Cata: Leonardo Castro 123clb.

Restaurante Botin: 70t.

Restaurante Horcher: 83bl.

Robert Harding Picture Library: Hugo Alonso 110-1; Walter Bibikow 4t; Barbara Boensch 2tr, 44-5; Jeremy Bright 37crb; Adrian Dominguez 4cl; Elan Fleisher 3tr,132-3; Xavier Florensa 36-37c; Elena de Las Heras 1; Juergen Richter 11b, 12crb; Arturo Rosas 4cr; White Star/Monica Gumm 4clb, / Alberto Mateo 32-3.

Salvador Bachiller: 122t.

SuperStock: age fotostock 10cla, 40br, 120tl; Album/Joseph Martin 16-7, /Oronoz Descalzas Reales-Coleccion, Madrid *Retrato del Infante Don Fernando* (1577) by Alonso Sanchez Coello 25cl; Classic Vision/age fotostock/Museo de la Real Academia de Bellas Artes de San Fernando *Self-portrait Goya at 69 years of age* by Francisco de Goya y Lucientes 19tl;

Fine Art Images/Museo del Prado *The Third of May 1808* (1814) by Francisco de Goya 19b, *The Three Graces* (16350 by Pieter Paul Rubens, c. 20cb, *Parnassus* (1631) by Nicolas Poussin 21b; LOOK-foto 10br; Marka 25cr; Joseph Martin 10cl; Oronoz 120br; Peter Barritt 40cl, 42tc; Robert Harding Picture Library 128crb; Travel Library Limited 11cb; Peter Willi/ El Escorial *The Martyrdom of Saint Mauritius* (1580-1) by El Greco 42c.

Taberna de Antonio Sanchez: 68b, Picasa117cb.

Teatro Real: Javier del Real 64b, 102bl.

The Bridge: Gonzalo Ayarra Burgos 105clb.

Velas de la Ballena: 123ca.

Xanadu: 59tl.

Cover
Front and spine - **Dreamstime.com:** Dennis Dolkens. Back - **Dreamstime.com:** Vichie81.

Pull Out Map Cover
Dreamstime.com: Dennis Dolkens.
All other images © Dorling Kindersley
For further information see www.dkimages.com

As a guide to abbreviations in visitor information blocks: **Adm** = *admission charge;* **DA** = *disabled access;* **D** = *dinner;* **L** = *lunch.*

Printed and bound in China

First American Edition, 2003
Published in the United States by
DK Publishing, 345 Hudson Street,
New York, New York 10014

Copyright 2003, 2016 © Dorling
Kindersley Limited

A Penguin Random House Company

16 17 18 19 10 9 8 7 6 5 4 3 2 1

**Reprinted with revisions 2007, 2009,
2011, 2013, 2015, 2016**

Published in Great Britain by Dorling
Kindersley Limited.

A catalog record for this book is available
from the Library of Congress.

ISSN 1479-344X

ISBN 978 1 4654 4576 6

MIX
Paper from responsible sources
FSC™ C018179
www.fsc.org

SPECIAL EDITIONS OF DK TRAVEL GUIDES

DK Travel Guides can be purchased in bulk quantities at discounted prices for use in promotions or as premiums. We are also able to offer special editions and personalized jackets, corporate imprints, and excerpts from all of our books, tailored specifically to meet your own needs.

To find out more, please contact:

in the US
specialsales@dk.com

in the UK
travelguides@uk.dk.com

in Canada
specialmarkets@dk.com

in Australia
**penguincorporatesales@
penguinrandomhouse.com.au**

Phrase Book

In an Emergency

Help!	¡Socorro!	soh-koh-roh
Stop!	¡Pare!	pah-reh
Call…	¡Llame a…	yah-meh ah
…a doctor!	…un médico!	oon meh-dee-koh
…an ambulance!	…una ambulancia!	oonah ahm-boo-lahn-thee-ah
…the police!	…la policía!	lah poh-lee-thee-ah
…the fire brigade!	…los bomberos!	lohs bohm-beh-rohs
Where is…	¿Dónde está…	dohn-deh ehs-tah
…the nearest telephone?	…el teléfono más próximo?	ehl teh-leh-foh-noh mahs prohx-ee-moh
…the nearest hospital?	…el hospital más próximo?	ehl ohs pee-tahl mahs prohx-ee-moh

Communication Essentials

Yes	Sí	see
No	No	noh
Please	Por favor	pohr fah-vohr
Thank you	Gracias	grah-thee-ahs
Excuse me	Perdone	pehr-doh-neh
Hello	Hola	oh-lah
Goodbye	Adiós	ah-dee-ohs
Good night	Buenas noches	bweh-nahs noh-chehs
Morning	La mañana	lah mah-nyah-nah
Afternoon/Evening	La tarde	lah tahr-deh
Yesterday	Ayer	ah-yehr
Today	Hoy	oy
Tomorrow	Mañana	mah-nya-nah
Here	Aquí	ah-kee
There	Allí	ah-yee
What?	¿Qué?	keh
When?	¿Cuándo?	kwahn-doh
Why?	¿Por qué?	pohr-keh
Where?	¿Dónde?	dohn-deh

Useful Phrases

How are you?	¿Cómo está usted?	koh-moh ehs-tah oos-tehd
Very well, thank you	Muy bien, gracias	mwee bee-ehn grah-thee-ahs
Pleased to meet you.	Encantado de conocerle.	ehn-kahn-tah-doh deh thehr-leh
See you soon	Hasta pronto	ahs-tah-prohn-toh
That's fine	Está bien	ehs-tah bee-ehn
Where is/are…?	¿Dónde está/están…?	dohn-deh ehs-tah/ehs-tahn
How far is it to…?	Cuántos metros/kilómetros hay de aquí a…?	kwahn-tohs meh-trohs/kee-loh-meh-trohs eye deh ah-kee ah
Which way to…?	¿Por dónde se va a…?	pohr dohn-deh seh bah ah
Do you speak English?	¿Habla inglés?	ah-blah een-glehs
I don't understand	No comprendo	noh kohm-prehn-doh
Could you speak more slowly please?	¿Puede hablar más despacio por favor?	pweh-deh ah-blahr mahs dehs -pah-thee-oh pohr fah-vohr
I'm sorry	Lo siento	loh see-ehn-toh

Useful Words

big	grande	grahn-deh
small	pequeño	peh-keh-nyoh
hot	caliente	kah-lee-ehn-teh
cold	frío	free-oh
good	bueno	bweh-noh
bad	malo	mah-loh
well	bien	bee-ehn
open	abierto	ah-bee-ehr-toh
closed	cerrado	thehr-rah-doh
left	izquierda	eeth-key-ehr-dah
right	derecha	deh-reh-chah
straight on	todo recto	toh-doh rehk-toh
near	cerca	thehr-kah
far	lejos	leh-hohs
up	arriba	ah-ree-bah
down	abajo	ah-bah-hoh
early	temprano	tehm-prah-noh
late	tarde	tahr-deh
entrance	entrada	ehn-trah-dah
exit	salida	sah-lee-dah
toilet	servicios	sehr-bee-thee-ohs
more	más	mahs
less	menos	meh-nohs

Shopping

How much does this cost?	¿Cuánto cuesta esto?	kwahn-toh kwehs-tah ehs-toh
I would like…	Me gustaría…	meh goos-ta-ree-ah
Do you have…?	¿Tienen…?	tee-yeh-nehn
Do you take cards?	¿Aceptan tarjetas?	ah-thehp-tahn tahr-heh-tahs
What time do you open/close?	¿A qué hora abren/cierran?	ah keh oh-rah ah-brehn/thee-ehr-rahn
This one	Éste	ehs-teh
That one	Ése	eh-seh
expensive	caro	kahr-oh
cheap	barato	bah-rah-toh
size, clothes	talla	tah-yah
size, shoes	número	noo-mehr-oh
antiques shop	la tienda de antigüedades	tee-ehn-dah deh ahn-tee-gweh-dah-dehs
bakery	la panadería	pah-nah-deh-ree-ah
bank	el banco	bahn-koh
bookshop	la librería	lee-breh-ree-ah
cake shop	la pastelería	pahs-teh-leh-ree-ah
chemist's	la farmacia	ahr-mah-thee-ah
grocer's	la tienda de comestibles	tee-yehn-dah deh koh-mehs-tee-blehs
market	el mercado	mehr-kah-doh
newsagent's	el kiosko de prensa	kee-ohs-koh deh prehn-sah
post office	la oficina de correos	oh-fee thee-nah deh kohr-reh-ohs
shoe shop	la zapatería	thah-pah-teh-ree-ah
supermarket	el super-mercado	soo-pehr-mehr-kah-doh
travel agency	la agencia de viajes	ah-hehn-thee-ah -deh beeah-hehs

Sightseeing

art gallery	el museo de arte	moo-seh-oh deh ahr-teh
cathedral	la catedral	kah-teh-drahl
church	la iglesia, la basílica	ee-gleh-see-ah bah-see-lee-kah
garden	el jardín	hahr-deen
library	la biblioteca	bee-blee-oh-teh-kah
museum	el museo	moo-seh-oh
tourist information office	la oficina de turismo	oh-fee-thee nah deh too-rees-moh
town hall	el ayunta-miento	ah-yoon-toh mee-ehn-toh
bus station	la estación de autobuses	ehs-tah-thee-ohn deh owtoh-boo-sehs
railway station	la estación de trenes	ehs-tah-thee-ohn deh treh-nehs

Staying in a Hotel

Do you have a vacant room?	¿Tiene una habitación libre?	tee-eh-neh oo-nah ah-bee- tah-thee-ohn lee-breh
double room	habitación doble	ah-bee-tah-thee-ohn doh-bleh
with double bed	con cama de matrimonio	kohn kah-mah deh mah-tree-moh-nee-oh
twin room	habitación con dos camas	ah-bee-tah-thee-ohn kohn dohs kah-mahs

single room	habitación individual	ah-bee-tah-thee-ohn een-dee-vee-doo-ahl
room with a bath	habitación con baño	ah-bee-tah-thee-ohn kohn bah-nyoh
porter	el botones	boh-toh-nehs
key	la llave	yah-veh
I have a reservation	Tengo una habitación reservada	tehn-goh oo-na ah-bee-tah-thee-ohn reh-sehr-bah-dah

Eating Out

Have you got a table for…?	¿Tiene mesa para…?	tee-eh-neh meh-sah pah-rah
I want to reserve a table	Quiero reservar una mesa	kee-eh-roh reh-sehr-bar oo-nah mehr-sah
The bill	La cuenta	kwehn-tah
I am a vegetarian	Soy vegetariano/a	soy beh-heh-tah-ree-ah-no/na
waitress/ waiter	camarera/ camarero	kah-mah-reh-rah/ kah-mah-reh-roh
menu	la carta	kahr-tah
fixed-price menu	menú del día	meh-noo dehl dee-ah
wine list	la carta de vinos	kahr-tah deh bee-nohs
glass	un vaso	bah-soh
bottle	una botella	boh-teh-yah
knife	un cuchillo	koo-chee-yoh
fork	un tenedor	teh-neh-dohr
spoon	una cuchara	koo-chah-rah
breakfast	el desayuno	deh-sah-yoo-noh
lunch	la comida/ el almuerzo	koh-mee-dah/ ahl-mwehr-thoh
dinner	la cena	theh-nah
main course	el primer plato	pree-mehr plah-toh
starters	los entremeses	ehn-treh-meh-ses
dish of the day	el plato del día	plah-toh dehl dee-ah
coffee	el café	kah-feh
rare (meat)	poco hecho	poh-koh eh-choh
medium	medio hecho	meh-dee-oh eh-choh
well done	muy hecho	mwee eh-choh

Menu Decoder

al horno	ahl ohr-noh	baked
asado	ah-sah-doh	roast
el aceite	ah-thee-eh-teh	oil
las aceitunas	ah-thee-toon-ahs	olives
el agua mineral	ah-gwa mee-neh-rahl	mineral water
sin gas/con gas	seen gas/kohn gas	still/sparkling
el ajo	ah-hoh	garlic
el arroz	ahr-rohth	rice
el azúcar	ah-thoo-kahr	sugar
la carne	kahr-neh	meat
la cebolla	theh-boh-yah	onion
el cerdo	therh-doh	pork
la cerveza	thehr-beh-thah	beer
el chocolate	choh-koh-lah-teh	chocolate
el chorizo	choh-ree-thoh	spicy sausage
el cordero	kohr-deh-roh	lamb
frito	free-toh	fried
la fruta	froo-tah	fruit
los frutos secos	froo-tohs seh-kohs	nuts
las gambas	gahm-bahs	prawns
el helado	eh-lah-doh	ice cream
el huevo	oo-eh-voh	egg
el jamón serrano	hah-mohn sehr-rah-noh	cured ham
la langosta	lahn-gohs-tah	lobster
la leche	leh-cheh	milk
el limón	lee-mohn	lemon
la mantequilla	mahn-teh-kee-yah	butter
la manzana	mahn-thah-nah	apple
los mariscos	mah-rees-kohs	seafood
la naranja	nah-rahn-hah	orange
el pan	pahn	bread

el pastel	pahs-tehl	cake
las patatas	pah-tah-tahs	potatoes
el pescado	pehs-kah-doh	fish
la pimienta	pee-mee-ehn-tah	pepper
el plátano	plah-tah-noh	banana
el pollo	poh-yoh	chicken
el postre	pohs-treh	dessert
el queso	keh-soh	cheese
la sal	sahl	salt
la salsa	sahl-sah	sauce
seco	seh-koh	dry
el solomillo	soh-loh-mee-yoh	sirloin
la sopa	soh-pah	soup
la tarta	tahr-tah	pie/cake
el té	teh	tea
la ternera	tehr-neh-rah	beef
el vinagre	bee-nah-greh	vinegar
el vino blanco	bee-noh blahn-koh	white wine
el vino rosado	bee-noh oh-sah-doh	rosé wine
el vino tinto	bee-noh een-toht	red wine

Numbers

0	cero	theh-roh
1	uno	oo-noh
2	dos	dohs
3	tres	trehs
4	cuatro	kwa-troh
5	cinco	theen-koh
6	seis	says
7	siete	see-eh-teh
8	ocho	oh-choh
9	nueve	nweh-veh
10	diez	dee-ehth
11	once	ohn-theh
12	doce	doh-theh
13	trece	treh-theh
14	catorce	kah-tohr-theh
15	quince	keen-theh
16	dieciséis	dee-eh-thee-seh-ees
17	diecisiete	dee-eh-thee-see-eh-teh
18	dieciocho	dee-eh-thee-oh-choh
19	diecinueve	dee-eh-thee-nweh-veh
20	veinte	beh-een-teh
21	veintiuno	beh-een-tee-oo-noh
22	veintidós	beh-een-tee-dohs
30	treinta	treh-een-tah
31	treinta y uno	treh-een-tah ee oo-noh
40	cuarenta	kwah-rehn-tah
50	cincuenta	theen-kwehn-tah
60	sesenta	seh-sehn-tah
70	setenta	seh-tehn-tah
80	ochenta	oh-chehn-tah
90	noventa	noh-vehn-tah
100	cien	thee-ehn
101	ciento uno	thee-ehn-toh oo-noh
200	doscientos	dohs-thee-ehn-tohs
500	quinientos	khee-nee-ehn-tohs
700	setecientos	seh-teh-thee-ehn-tohs
900	novecientos	noh-veh-thee-ehn-tohs
1,000	mil	meel

Time

one minute	un minuto	oon mee-noo-toh
one hour	una hora	oo-na oh-rah
half an hour	media hora	meh-dee-a oh-rah
Monday	lunes	loo-nehs
Tuesday	martes	mahr-tehs
Wednesday	miércoles	mee-ehr-koh-lehs
Thursday	jueves	hoo-weh-vehs
Friday	viernes	bee-ehr-nehs
Saturday	sábado	sah-bah-doh
Sunday	domingo	doh-meen-goh

Street Index